Writing Brave Press
547 North Avenue, Suite #173
New Rochelle, NY 10801
www.writingbravepress.com

Distributed by IngramSpark

Cover and Text Design: Karinna Klocko
Copyeditor: Meghan Muldowney & Patricia Lemer
Author Photos: Annika Friedland

Library of Congress Cataloging-in-Publication Data available.
ISBN 978-1-7375639-5-2 (paperback)
ISBN 978-1-7375639-6-9 (ebook)

First Edition

Heather,

Thank you for all that you do for our kids! Love,

Brigette

A Mother's Guide Through Autism

Brigitte M. Volltrauer Shipman

Acknowledgments

This book is the result of my loving journey of autism with my son, *Joseph*. Without him, I would not have had the inspired life experience to write this book. The love I have for my son has been my greatest motivation.

I am grateful for the guidance, coaching, and friendship from **Brooke Adams Law** and **Meg Dippel** with Writing Brave Press. Thank you for the continued love and support that you have given me throughout the process. Your encouragement inspires and fuels me when I need it the most.

Thank you to **Patricia Lemer** for believing in this book to support other mother guides on the journey of autism. You have given me great insight through your editing to make this book what I had always hoped it would be, healing mothers' hearts.

Thank you to **Say Kubo** for the many authentic conversations that led to a clear vision of what this book's purpose is and the healing it will offer to other mother guides. What was once a thought has turned into purpose.

Thank you to **Kathy Arp** for your deep love and friendship. Through our beloved coffee talks, this book became a reality.

Thank you to **Heidi Volltrauer** for believing in this work. Thank you for your constant support and for helping me sort my thoughts into reality.

Thank you to my beloved family and friends who stood by us through our darkest days. Your love and support made our autism journey lighter and brighter.

Foreword
written by Joseph

Throughout my life, my mom has said that in the unknown space we all inhabit before being born, I chose her as a parent. Now, this could be because I don't remember this primordial choice, but I tend to feel that her being my mom was a matter of luck. Whether it was luck, choice, or otherwise, I certainly feel gratitude toward my origins as a human being.

Despite growing up in a culture that, at times, was repressive and dogmatic, I was raised by expressive and curious people, who indulged my own expression and curiosity. This environment is something I view as an incredible boon, especially for someone who is on the autism spectrum.

As I imagine most parents would have done, my parents went to great lengths to provide for this then little-known special need of mine...but my mom went further still. She not only searched the country for specialists who could help me, but also later founded an organization to help others. She spoke out so loudly that I appeared in our local newspaper. She was not only my first abode of comfort and support, but my first example of persistence, strength, and resilience. She was also an inspirational figure of advocacy and activism, and her actions led to my dedication to various causes.

One of my favorite examples of her persistence occurred when I was quite young, preparing to enter elementary school. As a former first grade teacher, she made sure I was in a position where my special needs would be met educationally and socially. To her, this meant I needed to be integrated into the regular classroom with other children my age, not isolated in a separate placement.

My mother was thrilled when my third-grade teachers recommended me for the gifted program, but the powers that be disagreed. They recommended the traditional route of placing me in isolated special education, since I had an Individualized

Educational Plan (IEP). This is a legal document that ensures schools address the needs of students with disabilities. This essentially meant (especially at this time and place) sweeping me under a rug, so I could be shielded from the glares of those who viewed me as undesirable. Their justification for this was an IQ test, indicating that I was at the lower end of the range of average intelligence. Fortunately, my mother prevailed, and I was placed in regular classrooms after a different IQ test placed me way above average. I don't have many regrets in life, but one is that I never got to see the look on the administrator's face when he saw the second test results and knew he couldn't get past my mother.

I believe that persistence is the main characteristic of my mother that led her to write this book. The fact is she will help people, no matter what it takes. This drive of hers has been present throughout my life. The story of this remarkable person I call "Mom" has been written down, primarily out of the hope that her stories of learning and striving could help others have an easier time dealing with their trials and tribulations, or "tsunamis" as she calls them.

My mother is truly a born teacher, but not in the common image of one who gives truth from on high. She is, as the late Bruce Lee once said, "…a guide, a pointer to the truth that each student must find for himself." Hopefully her stories and experiences will help guide you. They point to some helpful ways to go in your own life or in the life of someone you love. I, for one, am proof that this is a certain possibility.

This book is dedicated to my son Joseph with all my love, As well as to all Mother Guides.

—

Contents

Acknowledgements

Foreword

Introduction

1 Our Journey Begins

2 Our Signs and Denials

3 Pain

4 Stumbling Through Grief

5 The Journey to Understanding

6 Accepting That It's Okay to Not Be Okay

7 The Crazy Monkeys of Fear

8 Living Life as a Superhero

9 Rocking Advocacy with Kindness

10 Always A Mother Guide

11 Moving Forward with Self-Compassion

12 Gratitude and Reflection

References

Introduction

Mother's Guide Through Autism is a handbook to offer emotional support and the space for healing to mothers whose children have been diagnosed on the autism spectrum. My intention is to give you strong support and advice on your autism journey. I want to teach and coach as many moms as I can. As a mother, educator, teacher, author, and life coach myself, I know that there are many mothers who need support. I have needed support along the way. Through that support, I have built my resilience. I've found cherished friendships, resources, understanding, and love.

I have felt deep pain and grief, and I have found my way back to living with more joy and happiness than I ever thought was possible. When I first began my autism journey, I did not take the time to consider anything else other than finding therapies to help my son. I believe that there are many positive takeaways from this quest; there were also many dire consequences to my own personal health and happiness.

It wasn't until I became a life coach and started to heal my heart that I realized that I could have lived my life with more joy and love rather than fear, anxiety, and full-time stress.

The only time I slept deep and hard was when I was completely exhausted, and my body just gave out. As soon as I could raise my head up off the pillow, away I went until the next time exhaustion overtook me.

My immune system had finally had enough. As a result, I experienced many health issues, including a Type I Diabetes diagnosis which almost took my life at age 39. Diabetes has been life-altering and is something that I will need to manage for the rest of my life.

Even though diabetes was my wake-up call, I still didn't listen. I ate better and continued to work out, but there was a piece to the puzzle that I did not see, or at least I didn't want to see. I resisted my inner work like a true champion; I won the gold medal by avoiding my deep pain.

Life went on with many more challenges. Along the way I was hospitalized for full body hives, which was not a result of food allergies. The hives were symptoms of my frazzled nerves, constant anxiety, deep fears, and unending pain. My doctor said he had never seen a case as severe as mine. After a total of eight EpiPen shots, multiple steroids, and a strict watch over my diabetes, eventually the hives went away. While I dealt with my physical healing for several months, I still avoided the inner work of healing my heart.

One day I was looking through O Magazine and came across an article written by life coach Martha Beck. I loved how she presented various tools that she taught others, which led me to research what a life coach was. I thought to myself, "I want to be a life coach!" I had been an educator for over 20 years, and I was getting many signs from the universe that it was time for a change. Moving on to life coaching seemed perfect!

I enrolled in the Martha Beck Life Coach program, and my life changed. I not only morphed my well-tuned teaching skills into a new profession, but I also began to do the inner work that I had been avoiding for so long. Each week, as I applied Martha Beck's tools and methods to coaching my cohort friends and master coaches, and they to me, I grew. Yes, I became a practiced life coach as I grew as a person. Most importantly, I began to experience deep joy that I had not felt in 20 years.

Once I was officially certified as a Martha Beck Life Coach, I had to make the difficult decision of discovering my coaching niche. My advisers suggested that I offer coaching from a life experience with which I had struggled personally.

I strongly considered being a health coach, because of my struggles with diabetes. I also thought about becoming a fitness coach. I had a true passion for fitness; I had been a group fitness instructor and personal trainer for extra money, while I taught school and stayed home with my children. Then I had a conversation with a master coach, and I casually mentioned my deep passion for helping mothers who were struggling with their children's autism diagnoses. But I felt like that work was still so big and heavy, and just too hard, even though I had done a lot of work around my pain. I just found myself shutting down when becoming an autism mom coach came up.

So, I chose health and wellness as my niche, because it seemed like an easier fit for me at the time. But as I moved forward with success as a health and wellness coach, I kept getting messages from the universe about being an autism coach. I ignored them and kept moving forward.

The messages got louder and more frequent. Some came from random conversations with people I had not spoken to or seen in years. One day I received an unexpected beautiful gift from a high school classmate's mother: a framed, colorful, cross-stitch plaque of the word AUTISM. Each letter had an acronym that spelled out a beautiful message.

It included the traditional autism puzzle piece symbol and a purple hand with the word "Believe" next to it.

My friend's mother told me that this gift was to thank me for doing so much in our community supporting families who had struggled with autism diagnoses. I was humbly surprised and thanked her for this heartfelt gift.

To me, the most fascinating part of this story is that I had not been active with my work in the autism community for at least 15 years. I started in 1998, and here it was 2016 when I received this gift! Yes, during more recent years, I had spoken to many mothers about autism, and my son Joseph and I had promoted an autism support group in 2010, but I was not really active with this work for a long time.

A few days later, a retired teacher I knew came up to me at the gym to tell me how proud she was of Joseph. She had been one of Joseph's teachers in eighth grade. Because she also had a special education background, she gave Joseph the guided support he needed desperately at that time in his life. Joseph was working at one of our local radio stations, and she said she loved listening to him. She was over the moon and one of Joseph's biggest fans.

This teacher then asked me what I was doing now. She passionately suggested that I write an autism curriculum for our state; she had contacts who would listen to me. She believed that Joseph was a success story that needed to be heard. She wanted me to share what I had done to bring my son from being incredibly dependent to being independent and working at a radio station. She marveled at his talent and how inspired she felt when she heard him deliver announcements, commercials, and her personal favorite, the news.

I left that conversation in shock...realizing, perhaps, that I needed to listen to these messages. Were they just coincidences? It certainly didn't feel like it to me. I went home and asked Joseph if he would be interested in working together in creating a podcast to help other mothers gain knowledge, hope, and inspiration. He listened and with his calm demeanor said, "I'll get back to you." I understood that this meant that he might have an answer in a few days, months, or even years, so I decided to give him some time and check in with him in a few days.

When I went back to Joseph and asked him about our potential partnership, he was then prepared to give me his answer. He had researched how to start a podcast, obtain the needed equipment, and how to record each episode. His answer was, "Yes." He shared what he knew with me, and we began planning when and how we would record our first episode. I had also just hired a Virtual Assistant to help us launch our new adventure. Now we just needed a name for our podcast.

I went on many meditation walks to help create the name of our podcast and some inspirational names came up, but they just didn't feel right. I decided to go to Joseph for creative help. After all, he was the reason I was even doing this work. He was my complete incentive.

I clearly remember coming in from my walk to ask him what he thought the name of our podcast could be. As I called for him, he walked out of his room upstairs and looked down at me to see what I needed from him. I asked him, "When you think of me as your mother on your journey of autism, what have I been to you?"

He paused, and his first response was, "Well, I'm blank." I know by now not to take an answer like this personally, because Joseph always speaks the truth. About ten seconds of silence passed and then he said, "Well, I see a wise old man sitting on a mountain with a long gray beard." He motioned his hands as if he were stroking the long greybeard.

"Oh," I said, "that's pretty cool."

He then came back with his final reply. "Really it's more like you are my tour guide."

"You mean in your life?" I asked.

He said, "Yes, you have shown me how."

A tour guide of life. Wow, I thought to myself, that's powerful and a great metaphor. In fact, I have been his tour guide when I needed to redirect him with love, patience, and communication.

Mother's Guide Through Autism is a result of that conversation. I listened to the one person who would know what a mother has been throughout his life: my son, who is my teacher, my world of wonder and joy. He inspired not only the name of a podcast, but also a coaching business and now a book.

I hope this book gives you a safe place to be completely honest with yourself. To unveil feelings that you have yet to discover. To understand your emotions and why you feel the way you do without guilt and self-judgment.

This is a place for you to heal with support and love waiting for you as you move forward on your journey as a mother guide. This book is all about you, the mother guide.

Apply this guide to your own personal experiences, pain, and healing. We all can relate and support each other which is an essential piece to our healing, but at the end of the day, this is you and your heart.

Trust the process and honor yourself as you move through this guide. When it begins to feel too big, just take a breath and step away until you are ready to move forward. There is no right or wrong way to heal. Throughout the exercises that I offer you, I'll ask you to check in with yourself each and every time. This is one of the daily tools I use for myself and when I coach other mother guides. The phrase "Meet Yourself Where You Are At" will become something you will apply to your healing.

The reason I would like for you to check in with yourself is to work at your own pace of healing. If something feels too big, then we may risk opening the door to fleeing and doing nothing. Healing in itself is big. There is no exact blueprint that each person can use. We all must use our own blueprint. This is as unique as each of our fingerprints.

This is the blueprint of healing that I personally discovered for myself. I have restructured it to fit as many mothers' hearts as possible. For some of you, this book will be a daily read and healing application. For others, it might be a book to use and then put down. I want to make it clear that any way you use this book is perfect. It is perfect because you will choose how it works for you. To meet yourself where you are at any given moment. I look forward to sharing my heart with your heart.

I want to disclose that I am still on my own autism journey as a mother guide. I will be a mother guide for the rest of my life. As I move forward, my intentional purpose is to continue to share my story and pay it forward with what I have learned. I am a teacher at heart, so this is my love language to teach, guide, and continue learning.

May you find peace and healing as you move through this healing guide. This is a prayer I wrote to use whenever you are losing hope, and you find yourself on your knees.

Mother Guide's Prayer

I pray from the depth of my mother's soul
To release my child from suffering,
To release my heart from deep sorrow and fear for
our future,
To send earth angels to guide us on our long journey,
To keep my mind, body and spirit filled with hope as I go through
my life guiding my child's disabilities and gifts.
May others who judge me be forgiven as I have been forgiven.
Give me the strength and courage to be the mother guide my
child needs when needed, and the intuition to allow them to fly to
their own destiny. Please guide my child with love and patience, all
the while guiding me, my child's Mother Guide

– Amen.

Written by Brigitte M. Volltrauer Shipman - Joseph's Mother Guide

1

Our Journey Begins

As I share my personal beginning of becoming a mother guide with you, I can only imagine that you will be able to relate to my story of becoming a mother for the first time. My husband and I were so excited when I found out that I was pregnant with our first child, because we both were ready to become parents.

I can vividly remember waiting for the lines on the pregnancy test to confirm what I intuitively already knew: I was pregnant. I can also still feel those butterflies in my stomach each and every time I announced with pure joy, "I'm going to have a baby."

We had so much fun telling our parents and close friends that we were going to start our family. Everyone who heard the news congratulated us, and we celebrated our baby with great joy and anticipation.

Reflecting on your own journey, how did you feel? Were you excited? Scared? Worried? Each journey begins differently. For me, it was a positive experience. I know that fear of the unknown can also be a part of this experience. I did become fearful when I realized that at some point my baby was going to come out of me. However, I was not thinking about that just yet.

I was teaching first grade at the time and my coworkers were excited for me. I received so much love and advice from them all. I listened to them and took most of their advice, but since I had never experienced being pregnant, I put some suggestions up on a shelf and moved forward.

I was about six months along when a friend of ours had her son. I went to the hospital to see her and her newborn baby, and that's when I had the realization that I too was going to give birth soon. She had a hard time with her delivery and looked exhausted; she warned me about what was to come. I spent the rest of the evening in fear of giving birth. I pulled out my copy of What to Expect When You're Expecting when I got home and tried to find some soothing words to lift my fears.

Everyone is different. Some have read everything on the subjects of birth and motherhood, others a little, and yet others virtually nothing during this phase of the journey. Luckily, I had a great deal of support from both books and people to alleviate my worries.

As I got closer to my due date, my belly got bigger by the minute. By the time I walked with a waddle, my nesting instincts were very strong. My mother told me not to worry about giving birth, because I would become ready naturally. I think that what she meant was that I would be so big and uncomfortable that I would look forward to giving birth. She wasn't wrong.

We decided that we wanted to know the sex of our baby. We had a hunch it was a boy, and we were right. Back then we didn't have gender reveal parties, but we did share our ultrasound photos with our close friends and family. Our baby looked healthy and that was what we wanted to hear more than anything. We had decided that even if the ultrasound showed any disabilities that I would deliver our child. That was our choice, but I was beyond thankful that I did not have to make that difficult decision because our baby was healthy.

We had a hunch it was a boy, and we were right.

___

I was so excited about decorating the nursery. I picked out the furniture and wallpaper. I arranged and rearranged everything until I felt it permeated with my heart. I rocked in the rocking chair that I would soon cradle my son in, and I felt my dream of becoming a mother coming true.

I was the guest of honor at several baby showers. We received so many beautiful gifts, and we knew that we were supported and loved. We also knew that this love was not just for us, but also for our son. To say "life was good" is a huge understatement.

We were ready by Joseph's due date of April 6th, but our son was not yet ready to enter the world. The doctor said it was normal for first pregnancies to be a few days late. I left each weekly doctor's visit disappointed. I was way past ready to deliver our son. All the fear of labor and delivery had left me, just as my mother predicted. I was truly huge and truly miserable physically. I waited for any sign of one single labor pain. But I experienced it for another 10 days.

Finally, on April 16, 1992, I woke up around 2:00 a.m., and knew, without a doubt, it was time. I was so thankful to feel my first labor pain, because I was going to be induced in the next couple of days if Joseph hadn't come naturally.

I immediately got out of bed, and I tried to remember the breathing techniques that I learned in our Lamaze classes. I took a shower, woke my husband, and told him it was time. He shot up out of the recliner he had fallen asleep in, as if the house were on fire. We grabbed what we had pre-packed for the hospital two weeks earlier, and off we went. We were so excited. The day had finally come on which we would meet our son.

As I was being wheeled into the delivery room, I looked up and through a big window, I peered at a crowd of familiar faces. There was our family, friends, and even some people I was surprised to see. We lived in a small town, and I was thrilled to know that the birth of our firstborn was a true event. The nurse asked me with a surprised tone if I was aware of how many people were there waiting for our son to be born. I smiled for just a moment, and then quickly went back to focusing on giving birth. After twelve hours of labor, and two hours of pushing, Joseph made his appearance. He was the most popular baby born that day in a small-town hospital with more love than most people receive in a lifetime.

I immediately held Joseph in my arms, and he looked right into my eyes. I asked his father, "Did you see that?" He replied, "Yes, I saw that." It was a magical, meaningful, knowing moment that was bigger than the three of us.

My husband looked at Joseph and me in those first precious moments of parenthood and declared, "You know, I read somewhere that children pick their parents. I think he is letting us know that he picked us." I love that idea. I do believe that in those first moments, when our eyes locked, Joseph let us know that. What we never anticipated was that we were about to have an adventure that most people just hear about. Maybe Joseph was saying, "Hi Mom. We have a lot of work to do here, and it's all going to be okay."

I personally believe that, yes, he was letting me know many things. I received his messages with a love that was almost more than my heart could hold. This love consumed my entire mind, body, and soul. It was an all-consuming love. In one moment, I knew what my purpose was in my life. I was a mother. I now had superhero powers. I was without these powers until that very moment. I just knew that being a mother was bigger than me; it was my purpose.

I then handed my baby boy back to the nurse, and I felt the greatest joy and relief all at the same time. The feeling I had at that moment was heavenly...beyond what I could have ever imagined.

The next couple of days in the hospital were all about Joseph and me getting acquainted. When the day came for us to leave, I was ready but also fearful. I had no clue of what to do. My husband and I decided to go stay with my parents for a few days, until I was feeling stronger. That was one of the best decisions I ever made.

On day four, Joseph's everything changed. Joseph went from fairly content to crying nonstop. My mother, husband, and I took shifts caring for our son. We couldn't figure out what had changed because we were doing everything the same. What would have caused him to cry inconsolably?

I didn't know at the time that this was the beginning of my autism journey. We immediately started researching colicky babies. We went down the list of suggested changes to find a solution. We were all exhausted. I believed that I had a baby with colic and that it would pass sooner or later.

A few days later, one of my best friends gave me some advice. Her brother found that when he tried white noise, such as a vacuum cleaner, his newborn baby stopped crying. As soon as I got off the phone, I shared this with my mother and husband. We got out the vacuum cleaner and turned it on. The three of us watched with anticipation, and almost immediately, Joseph stopped crying. We were elated, exhausted, and afraid to put him down.

It's an awful feeling to be afraid of putting your baby down to sleep. I knew as soon as he woke up, we would have to try to calm him again. The nonstop crying was beyond anything I had ever experienced. To say it was hard is an understatement!

I am sure you can remember a time when you began your own personal journey as a mother guide, but you just didn't know it. It isn't something that happens overnight. At this point, I just knew babies can be colicky and it would eventually pass.

As long as the vacuum cleaner hummed, Joseph slept. This new discovery was beyond life-changing in those early days. But once we caught our breath, we realized that using a vacuum cleaner a couple of hours a day as a pacifier was not going to work long-term.

I was filled with mixed emotions as we prepared to leave my parents' home. At least I had one tool, the vacuum, to calm our colicky baby. Thank goodness that when we got settled in our own home, Joseph seemed calmer. We thought that perhaps the formula changes we had made and the quieter setting helped him cope better. I can remember my husband mowing the lawn as I put Joseph down for a nap that afternoon. I thought to myself, "We got this parent thing." All is well.

Within an hour, the crying began again. My heart sank into my stomach. We got out the vacuum, and made a cassette tape recording of the vacuum noise. Unfortunately, we recorded over one of our favorite dance groups at the time, Bel Biv Devoe, so when side one ran out of the vacuum recording, their hit song "Poison" blared through the speaker. It's a funny memory to me now. It would have been so simple to record the vacuum to the other side of the tape, but back then we were in panic mode and not thinking clearly.

Joseph continued with periods of nonstop crying for an endless, challenging first three months of his life. The good news was that he seemed to become more consistent with his schedule, and we felt like he was thriving. We figured out that the key to keeping him calm was to adhere to a strict schedule. As soon as we veered off his schedule, he started crying. It could then take hours of trying every trick in the book to calm him down.

After endless discussions, we decided that I would take a one-year leave of absence from teaching to stay home with Joseph. I loved teaching, but I knew this decision would be best for our son. He needed that strict schedule to keep him from spiraling into nonstop crying. The only people who we felt could help us at that time were both of our mothers, who were our support system when we needed a few hours or an evening to get out of the house.

I wrote down a very detailed schedule to make sure that Joseph stayed happy and could fall asleep. If he missed that magical time to eat or nap, the crying began. Once he went past a certain point, it was almost impossible to soothe him because he was so overstimulated. I was a mother who documented everything. I had gotten a calendar with stickers to record Joseph's first year of life as a gift from one of my baby showers. I loved it! I wrote the highlighted moments of each day down.

I was so glad that I recorded these important moments, because now they help tell our story as I look back on the unique development of my son.

Here are a few highlights from Joseph's first year

April 16: Baby arrives

April 18: Left the hospital and went to (my parents) Oma and Ota's house.

April 19: First Easter. You cried all night. We love you!

April 24: We all came home!

—

Most of May through July are blank, because Joseph cried through most of those days. These were such challenging days, but by August, most of our days were filled with family, friends, and lots of love.

By 6 months, Joseph was crawling. By 9 months, he was walking mostly by himself, but needed some help. At 10 months, he was walking independently.

At 11 months, I wrote this note in his calendar.

Funny things you said and did

You love music! When you hear music, you dance a lot and you sing la la la! When we laugh, you laugh or fake laugh.

—

Special personality traits

You are very stubborn! You want your way and don't stop trying to get it. You know how to make people laugh! You also love people and like to study them.

At 12 months, Joseph was thriving. We celebrated his first birthday with so many friends and family. He loved people and most foods; by all indicators, he was advanced in all developmental markers.

Although I didn't understand for years that Joseph was showing signs of Autism Spectrum Disorder (ASD), I knew deep in my heart that something wasn't "normal" in his development. My reasoning was that he was a genius, and this is why he was so "sensitive" to his surroundings. Reflecting about the beginning of my journey has helped me understand more about my experience as a mother guide. It also is an important part of opening your heart to begin healing.

Reflect on YOUR experience. Clearly, this reflection is optional, just as are all the exercises in this book. Take three big beautiful breaths, and meet yourself where you are right now. If you feel like you are ready to answer some questions, then grab something to write with, your favorite journal, or, if you prefer, write your answers here in the mother's guide book.

If you are not yet ready to write, then just keep reading on, or go do something kind for yourself. Either way, I am so grateful that you have picked up this book.

If you are an adoptive, surrogate, or foster parent, or of any gender, these reflection questions are for you too. In my mind, you are a mother guide just as any birth mother is. Being a mother cannot be defined. Although a mother has been traditionally defined as a woman who gives birth to a baby, I do not believe that this definition is totally accurate.

We all have our own personal ideas of what motherhood is or can be. Often it comes from what we have experienced and learned from our own mothers. I know what it feels like to be a mother, but it is hard to define. I am not a huge advocate for putting labels or people in boxes. Being a mother is a feeling! You will have your own idea or experience of what being a mother is and that is beautiful!

I once coached a surrogate mother who had so many deep feelings that she wasn't her child's mother. This woman was very courageous, and we worked together defining what a mother is. After we went through this work, she realized that not only was she a mother, she was an exceptional mother.

My Mother's Guide Journey Begins

What were you feeling when you discovered that you were going to be a mother? Were you excited, surprised, shocked, scared, alone, supported?

_____

_____

_____

_____

_____

_____

_____

_____

_____

_____

Who was your support system? Your family? Friends? Your
spouse or partner? Work family? Medical professionals?
A kind stranger?

_____

_____

_____

_____

_____

_____

_____

How did you know they supported you?
How did they show support?

_____

_____

_____

_____

What was your expectation of being a mother? What visions of
motherhood did you have?

_____

_____

_____

_____

_____

What was your greatest challenge while you were pregnant or waiting for your child to arrive? What was challenging about it? Maybe you didn't have any, so you can skip this one.

_____

_____

_____

_____

_____

_____

_____

How did you prepare for motherhood? Books, research, mentors' advice, or did you wing it?

_____

_____

_____

_____

What were your first moments of motherhood like?

_____

_____

_____

_____

Tell the story of meeting your child for the first time:

Thinking back, did you have any early signs that your child might be autistic? If so, what were they?

_____

_____

_____

_____

_____

_____

Let's take a moment and check in. If you can't remember some of your journey, no worries. Do your best to answer these questions. The point is to reflect and open your heart to the beginning of your journey. If your heart is in a good place, and you are feeling joy and love for your child, then read on.

If you have any negative feelings that might be lingering, here is an exercise to help you release the "icky" feelings and let your love for your child pour in. Take a moment from your heart space, and write your own definition of what a mother is to you. List some of the qualities that make a good mother.

SPACE FOR THOUGHTS

My hunch is that you are the mother that you just defined. You have the qualities of being a good mom, even a great mom. Feel that feeling and know that you are doing your best in each moment. Give yourself grace by appreciating all that you do and are for your child. Celebrate your motherhood. How? In a way that feels like you are giving yourself deep kindness. That can look as unique as motherhood.

The mother guide's prayer is useful any time you feel negative feelings. Find a quiet place and pray this prayer. This will offer you peace.

Mother Guide's Prayer

I pray from the depth of my mother's soul
To release my child from suffering,
To release my heart from deep sorrow and fear for
our future,
To send earth angels to guide us on our long journey,
To keep my mind, body and spirit filled with hope as I go through
my life guiding my child's disabilities and gifts.
May others who judge me be forgiven as I have been forgiven.
Give me the strength and courage to be the mother guide my
child needs when needed, and the intuition to allow them to fly to
their own destiny. Please guide my child with love and patience, all
the while guiding me, my child's Mother Guide

– Amen.

Written by Brigitte M. Volltrauer Shipman - Joseph's Mother Guide

▬

This is also a time to acknowledge that you are a mother guide and you are specially made for your child. Take a moment for yourself and allow the power of motherhood into your heart.

Now take a moment and write your own Mother Guide's Prayer for you and your child. You may refer to prayer as meditation. Put this into your own words for your personal mother's guide journey. Motherhood is unique and beautiful.

Mother Guide's Prayer or Meditation:

_____

_____

_____

_____

_____

_____

_____

_____

_____

_____

_____

_____

_____

_____

_____

_____

Use your Mother Guide's Prayer or Meditation as often as you need as you continue on your journey of healing your heart.

2

Signs and Denials

Around Joseph's first birthday, we realized that our son's development was imbalanced. In some areas, he was very advanced, naming animals, recognizing shapes, and completing difficult puzzles. However, his language and social interaction seemed to lag. How could he be so advanced and so behind in his child development? It made no sense to me.

We were still unconcerned. After all, accoring to the research, many highly intelligent people had delayed speech. I read that Albert Einstein didn't speak until the age of four. Interestingly enough, years later, I learned that although Einstein did not have a formal autism diagnosis, many believe he was "on the spectrum."

As I continued to observe my son, I felt deep down inside that something was causing his speech delay, his tantrums, his lag in potty training, his unexplained fears, obsessive behaviors, and lack of interest in other children. I can remember the day I took Joseph to the park to play with other children. I was feeling the need to expand his world so that he had more opportunities to experience play with his peers. I thought that maybe he was behind socially because he was not around other children enough.

I loaded him up and off we went to have a beautiful afternoon full of fun. He started by playing with gravel. He picked it up and dropped it onto a dinosaur statue over and over again.

Then, out of nowhere, another boy came over and squatted down next to Joseph. He simply smiled and began to pick the gravel up and put it on the dinosaur statue, just as Joseph had done. Joseph took one look at him, screamed, and ran away.

The boy's mother, who was standing close by, looked over at me confused. I just smiled and explained that Joseph was just learning how to play with others. I then walked over to comfort my son. I told him it was okay to play with the other little boy, but Joseph wanted nothing to do with him.

I remember the sinking feeling in my gut...an intuitive "knowing" deep inside of me that something was not right with my son. It was so confusing. My mixed feelings were empathy for the other little boy who Joseph had screamed at. Embarrassment for his mother, whose son had tried to befriend my son. Anger and frustration at myself and Joseph, that my son had behaved this way. Why couldn't I figure out this crazy puzzle of delays and giftedness that my child was displaying?

A few weeks later, my husband and I were watching television while Joseph was playing with some of his favorite toys. One of Joseph's obsessions was watching the same videos over and over. He noticed that each of the letters F.H.E. on the logo of his beloved Family Home Entertainment videos were a different color. As we watched in amazement, Joseph suddenly wrote the logo F.H.E. over and over again with his tiny pointer finger, while whispering the letters to himself as he wrote. His reproduction of the logo looked identical to the one on the video cover. I then had a lightning bolt of clarity that hit me from out of nowhere. In one of my college child development classes, I had heard the word "autism." I looked up at my husband and said, "Do you think Joseph has autism?" We both looked at our son writing the logo on the carpet over and over again. We looked back up at each other and almost simultaneously said, "No, that doesn't make any sense."

Next, he painted the logo F.H.E. on his art paper, while sitting in his adjustable high chair that transformed into a very nice toddler desk. I can still see him clearly dipping his paintbrush in each of the three logo letter colors. He had a precise peripheral slant with his eyes. Then he closely navigated the paintbrush to touch down into the primary color plastic tray palette. He was very exact with each stroke of his paintbrush. He painted each letter as an exact replica of the Family Home Entertainment logo.

Were the signs of autism present each and every day? Yes, they were, but when you love your child more than your own life, it is so easy to ignore them. All I knew about autism at that time was that if my son was indeed autistic, our world would come crashing down all around us.

In my eyes, Joseph continued to thrive in his artistic abilities, knowledge of numbers, letters, and even reading words, singing, and acting to the exact timing of each of his beloved videos. However, he also was not using his vocabulary words in proper sentence structure. He still required a strict schedule, had adversity to certain foods (mainly potatoes), and was happiest at home or with his grandparents. We were still holding onto hope that Joseph would wake up one day and just begin talking like so many friends and family had predicted he would. I believed deeply that this miracle could happen, and I prayed each day that my son would be okay and that his genius-like behavior was the cause of the developmental delays.

Over the past few decades, many mothers have reached out to me. I listen carefully to their questions, and I hear the same tone of hope in their voices that I had, that it isn't autism. I was that mom. It didn't matter who I was asking. I just wanted to hear them say that whatever behavior Joseph was displaying, it couldn't be a lifelong disability. My heart was hanging on a string.

If you are a mother guide in this stage of your journey, you will be okay no matter what the diagnosis ends up being. No matter where you are on your journey, my hunch is that the signs have always been present, right along with the powerful denial. I believe that denial steps in when the pain of our reality is just too great to bear. I was not ready to dive into what my gut was telling me long before my mind could comprehend my reality. My reality is that my son was in fact autistic. As soon as I would go to the possibility of that diagnosis, my mind would instantly grasp for data to prove that he was not.

According to the Mayo Clinic Staff and their article, "Adult Health," in Healthy Lifestyle Magazine, understanding denial and its purpose will help you get to the other side.

When you are in denial, you:

• Can't acknowledge a difficult situation

• Try not to face the facts of a problem

• Downplay possible consequences of the issue

A short period of denial can actually be helpful, because it gives your mind the opportunity to unconsciously absorb shocking or distressing information at a pace that won't send you into a psychological tailspin. However, if denial persists, and prevents you from taking appropriate action, then it can be a harmful response that inhibits you from reaching out and getting the medical help and therapies you and your child need. The autism journey can be a roller coaster ride of emotions, and denial is certainly one of those powerful emotions.

If you fear the possibility that your child has ASD, and you could possibly be in denial, then take a big beautiful breath, and answer these questions. If you feel like answering these questions is too big right now, then come back to this later. Meet yourself where you are at this moment.

Does your child have signs of ASD? What signs are you observing?

_____

_____

_____

_____

_____

_____

_____

_____

When you look at the signs of ASD that your child displays, what happens inside your gut and brain? Do you shift your mind to observed data that they are not autistic? Check into your body. Do you get a feeling in your body that lets you know that this is the truth? (Examples include: chest tightening, feeling a punch in the gut, tears of emotion, to name a few.) Take your time and just write down what you notice in your mind and body.

When I think about my child being on the ASD lifelong journey, I notice my mind...

SPACE FOR THOUGHTS

When I think about my child being on the ASD lifelong journey, I notice what in my body? Describe what you are feeling and where it is located.

_____

_____

_____

_____

_____

_____

_____

What is your biggest fear about being a mother guide on the autism journey?

_____

_____

_____

_____

_____

_____

_____

_____

_____

_____

Allow yourself to fully express your fears and emotions. Writing them down on paper can help you sort and navigate your deepest feelings. I know this can be difficult, so be gentle and kind with yourself as you journal.

_____

_____

_____

_____

_____

_____

_____

_____

_____

_____

_____

_____

_____

_____

_____

_____

_____

Go back and read what you wrote about your deepest fears and emotions. Are there any fears that are irrational? Your deepest fear may be caused by a belief that simply is not true.

What fears or beliefs do you have that are irrational or not true?

_____

_____

_____

_____

_____

_____

_____

The journey of autism is uncertain. You do not know without a doubt that this fear or belief will be true. That is what fear is. Fear is an emotion that comes up when we feel something is dangerous or may cause us deep pain. Take comfort for now that this irrational belief or fear is not present today. Take a breath and recite this phrase or mantra: All is well at this moment. Go back to this mantra or phrase when you feel your fear creeping back in.

Great job identifying your fearful beliefs. We will dive deeper into dissolving these fears later in Chapter 7. For now, go do something kind for yourself.

My small act of kindness today is:

_____

_____

_____

_____

_____

3

Pain

Months passed, and my husband and I decided to enroll Joseph in a trusted local daycare I worked at when I was in college. Our goal was to prepare him for kindergarten, especially in the areas of speech and social skills. The first day I left Joseph at daycare, I felt like I was abandoning my son in a strange land that spoke a different language. I had to keep reminding myself that I was only leaving him for a couple of hours to play with other children, and that the experience would be good for him. Instead of driving right home, I went around the block, so I could see what Joseph decided to do after I left. As I turned the corner in anticipation of seeing him playing with the other kids, my heart sank into the pit of my stomach. There stood Joseph, looking SO lost, in the exact place I had left him.

I felt like a giant fist had punched me in the gut. I sobbed and sobbed as I watched my sweet, immobilized boy just standing there. I instantly called my husband and told him what I had witnessed. He assured me that we were doing the right thing. We both knew that we had to introduce Joseph into the bigger world in which he would be participating.

Within a week, I received a phone call requesting that I speak to the speech pathologist. She recommended that Joseph be evaluated for delayed language development.

Having taught first grade, this request neither concerned nor surprised me. I was aware that Joseph was socially delayed and had little sentence structure. He was echolalic, which simply means that he repeated whatever he heard someone say. For example, if I asked, "Do you want juice?", he would reply,

"Do you want juice?" He had little expressive language of his own. My expectation was that the testing would confirm the delays we were aware of and offer him speech therapy in order to catch up. But that's not what happened. In a short, direct follow-up conference about his test results, I heard four words that changed our lives forever: "Your son is autistic."

I don't even remember driving home; four words truly changed everything in an instant. I heard only a loud ringing in my ears, and I felt such deep pain in my heart that I feared it might kill me.

I tried to process the news, but just couldn't. I had heard it and felt it, yet did not understand it. I had listened to a dim prognosis based only on a short observation by someone who barely knew my son.

The next day, I gathered my courage and called the speech pathologist. I kept trying to wrap my brain around what an autism diagnosis really meant. She was very direct and informed me that she had years of experience working with children who were autistic. She explained that some were high-functioning and others low-functioning. She called it a spectrum and advised that Joseph was somewhere in the middle.

After pausing for a minute, she threw out the bomb. She said, "He will probably need to live with assistance when he becomes an adult." She added that, more than likely, Joseph would not be able to go to a traditional school. With each word that she spoke, I felt as if I was being beaten. My soul, my mother's heart, could not bear to hear what I was being told. I wanted her to stop, but I listened as she recommended that he have further testing at the Children's Hospital in Little Rock. I then shut down. I could not process any more information. I was numb.

The son that we had known for the past three years no longer existed. Our dreams for his life were shattered overnight. We were in shock. Our family and friends were in shock. When I looked at my son, I saw that he was still there; however, I felt like the son I had given birth to no longer existed.

In my profound pain, all I wanted to do was hold my baby and just sob for the loss of our sweet, innocent child. I could barely function from the pain I felt, not just in one location in my body, but everywhere. It consumed every breath I struggled to take, as I continuously sobbed.

Then, all of a sudden, almost magically, I comprehended the reality of it, and Joseph looked completely different to me. Even though my mind couldn't make any sense of what this meant, my heart told me that we were all going to suffer. I would suffer, because my child would suffer. I could now see that Joseph's life would be a struggle.

As we began this lifetime battle to save our son, the pain I felt in the next few weeks and months was so intense that it simply was not manageable. I was completely stricken and consumed with pain. I have often heard that sometimes words are not enough to truly express how one feels. I truly believe that language does not exist to explain the deep inner pain that I felt.

As I moved forward each day, my pain morphed into anger, which fueled me to find answers for my son. I became obsessed, and each day researched, called, and worked on how to get Joseph the therapies that he desperately needed. We lived in a small rural town and the resources and knowledge there were very limited.

Thankfully, we had family and friends who supported us in finding answers. We found a psychologist who diagnosed Joseph with Pervasive Developmental Disorder, Not Otherwise Specified (PDD-NOS). This term, while no longer used, was really helpful to us because it gave us hope. It meant that Joseph was on the high-functioning end of the autism spectrum. While he excelled in some areas, he struggled in others. He could read, sculpt, dance, paint, name every animal and shape, and count up to 100. Yet, his sensory processing skills, expressive language, motor skills, and social skills were all behind. Although hope presented itself, I was living with deep pain each and every day. I watched my son through the eyes of fear and longed for him to be happy and healthy, rather than standing alone and isolated in this world.

Pain has always been a part of my personal journey, as long as I can remember. This physical pain was especially hard to endure. At this part of my journey, I felt my deepest pain when I first heard the words that my son was autistic. There was so much going on in my body. The part of this pain that has stayed with me is the memory of the ringing in my ears. I lost my ability to do anything but sob. I didn't understand any of it. All I knew was that I was in deep physical pain. It was the kind of cry you experience in your sleep and you can't wake up…a complete nightmare.

I have gradually learned how important it is to go to your pain, although I know it is not something any of us want to do. I still do not like sitting with my pain, but what I have learned is that it is essential, and that each time I look my pain in the eyes it gets easier. I no longer feel that ache in my stomach. I know that my pain will eventually dissolve if I give it permission to be present. I am no longer fearful of letting pain hang out for a few hours. Over time, I have developed a relationship with my pain.

It's okay for pain to visit us throughout our journey. Pain serves a purpose. I know that may be hard to believe, but pain is here to teach us and allow us deep growth.

If you are in that deep pain right now, you may not be ready to befriend pain, learn from pain, or grow from pain. Feeling it can just be enough for now.

Moving forward, we will be working with your pain. If today is not the day for you to do this work, then please as always, meet yourself where you are at. If you aren't ready to do this practice, then come back to it when you are ready. Heal at your own pace. There are no rules to healing your heart.

What has caused you the deepest pain on your Mother Guide journey?

_____

_____

_____

_____

_____

_____

_____

_____

_____

_____

_____

_____

_____

_____

You will be able to unburden your pain little by little. Let's begin with this practice.

Journaling Practice: Find a safe peaceful space where you can spend the next 15 to 20 minutes answering these essential healing questions and journaling prompts. Remember when we resist, it persists, and when we feel, we heal.

Write about who your pain is, what it looks like.
Be as descriptive as you can be. Give every detail.

_____

_____

_____

_____

_____

_____

_____

_____

_____

_____

_____

_____

_____

_____

_____

_____

_____

_____

_____

_____

Name your pain: _____

Giving your pain a name can help you form a relationship with pain. It can also help you get rid of the fear of pain. Pain is an old friend who will always visit us. I named my pain the Wicked Witch Elphaba. She looks like the wicked witch of the West from the movie The Wizard of Oz. She swoops in out of nowhere when I least expect her to. I can be having a great day filled with sunshine. Then without notice, the sky becomes black, the wind begins to blow, and in an instant, she has consumed me. I usually feel her in my gut first. The familiar feeling of a sick knotted ball takes my stomach hostage. When this feeling comes to me, I recognize it and begin to speak to Elphaba.

"Hello, Elphaba. You are back, and I am not happy that you are back. Why are you here? What lesson am I not understanding?" Once I begin to address Elphaba, my stomach begins to feel better, and I begin to process what is going on that causes her to return to me. I also know that whatever the reason, it is necessary for me to move forward and learn. I am being pushed and the aha eventually comes. I do not fear her anymore. She has become a friend who hurts me deeply, but she also leads me through my pain to heal.

Now that you have described who your pain is, picture and feel your pain to answer these questions. As you write about your pain, replace pain with pain's name. Use your deepest pain.

I once heard that pain's purpose is to push us into growth as part of our human experience. When I first heard this idea, I was in a much better place with my pain, because I had done a lot of emotional work through my life coach training. Pain does push and teach us. As I have mentioned before, I learn best when I learn through pain. I now understand that pain does have purpose.

Think of how pain is pushing you to grow.

—

How does pain push me?

_____

_____

_____

_____

_____

_____

_____

What does pain teach me?

_____

_____

_____

_____

_____

_____

I dissolve my pain by talking to her or writing to her. I spend time with her, and then I ask her to go away until the next time. I picture Elphaba zooming away on her broomstick and getting smaller as she travels deep into the galaxy.

You can also dissolve your pain by visualizing pain getting smaller. Imagine placing pain in a box and putting the box on a shelf, or putting pain in a bottle and tightly sealing the opening. You choose what works for you, and how you want to dissolve your pain. Keep in mind that pain will return, but you now have tools of how to communicate, negotiate, and most importantly grow from this relationship.

How do you dissolve your pain?

_____

_____

_____

_____

_____

_____

_____

_____

_____

ROOM FOR DOODLES

↘

→

Knowing who your pain is will help bring the light. Wherever there is darkness, there is also light. We all need the tools and the courage to get through the darkness. You might have heard the phrase "behind the clouds, the sun is shining," which is absolutely true each and every time we see a cloudy dark sky. We just can't see the sun until the clouds dissipate.

It is essential that you give yourself loving kindness before moving on to Chapter 4.

4

Stumbling Through Grief

Grief is defined in the dictionary as "deep sorrow," especially when it is caused by someone's death. Elizabeth Gilbert in her book Eat, Pray, Love wrote, "Deep grief sometimes is almost like a specific location, a coordinate on a map of time. When you are standing in that forest of sorrow, you cannot imagine that you could ever find your way to a better place. But if someone can assure you that they themselves have stood in that same place, and now have moved on, sometimes this will bring hope."

My deep grief with my son's diagnosis has left some scars, but I have healed through my pain. I believe we can offer hope to each other when we have somehow gotten to the other side of grief. We can share our experiences in a way that allows others to see we were once there, on our knees, exactly where they are, and now we walk tall with hope once again.

I know that all mothers experience and live with grief on their journey as a mother guide of an autistic child. I also know that I was on my knees when my son Joseph was first diagnosed on the autistic spectrum. It is life-altering grief to hear those words about your child. No one wants to hear the "A word."

My grief was huge, messy, and painful. I have stumbled through my grief for many years. My hunch is that I will stumble again; however, I will be able to regain my balance faster next time, because I now know that grief is a part of being alive.

Grief has been studied to offer us knowledge, comfort, and hope. I have gotten to the other side of grief with my son's diagnosis and life with autism. I couldn't feel hope when I was in the middle of the forest without a compass. I had no direction. It was my first life experience of being lost in grief.

So, how do you find hope in this new world that feels over-whelming, when your mother's heart has been torn right out of your chest? Great question. It's hard, I know because I've been there. But I also know that we can find hope again, because I have done it, and I will continue to do it. Hope is the north star. When I found hope, I learned to hold on to it. I learned to follow hope to find my way out of the deep dark forest of grief.

Where did I find hope? In my son's smile, in my love for my beautiful child, in other mothers. Hope is all around. If you are in the deep darkness of the forest, just look up toward the light. Look for any signs of hope to get you moving forward.

Take a moment and look around you. Where is hope hiding in your life? This may feel like a scavenger hunt. Please don't stop until you find at least one sign of hope in your life.

___

Signs of Hope:

1.

2.

3.

4.

5.

I **HOPE** you found more than five signs of hope in your life. Take a look at your signs, and go deep into the feeling that hope offers you. When you get stuck or stumble in your own grief, go back to finding hope in your life. Remember that it is your north star, and it will guide you out of the dark days.

Grief has stages to travel through. If this is your first experience with stumbling through grief, you may recognize which one of these stages you are in. Understanding what is happening while you are walking through grief may help you find your balance and footwork without stumbling.

You can find many resources to educate yourself on the stages of grief. I have read many books about this subject. I recommend that if you would like to know more about the stages of grief to find a book or professional expert in grief. I did a bit of research which I am applying to this guide. Here are three books and authors that may be helpful:

> *On Grief & Grieving: Finding the Meaning*
> *of Grief Through the Five Stages of Loss*
> by Elisabeth Kubler-Ross, M.D. and David Kessler

> *A Grief Observed* by C.S. Lewis

> *Option B: Facing Adversity, Building*
> *Resilience, and Finding Joy*
> by Sheryl Sandberg and Adam Grant

As you move through this guide you may recognize the five stages of grief:

• Denial
• Anger
• Bargaining
• Depression
• Acceptance

During my journey as a mother guide, I experienced all five stages at some point. I have also been in more than one stage of grief at a time, depending on what was happening at any given moment.

Grief is a part of life, but how we get through it, or don't get through it, determines how you live the rest of your life. It takes a great deal of courage, work, support, and the willingness to accept the process. It is by far the hardest thing I have ever done.

Grief can become an old friend who pops in and out of your life once you lean into it. Sounds like you want to run, right? It's natural to run away. Why? Because it hurts like hell. Feeling pain is part of finding your way out of the dark forest. You have begun a relationship with your own personal pain, which is part of your grief.

For now, there is no pressure or hurry to move through your grief. This is the beauty of owning your own personal journey. There is no right or wrong way to grieve. I will be open and vulnerable in sharing my journey of healing to offer you support on your journey. The previous chapters and the next few chapters are all about experiencing grief while still living my life.

I am going to ask you to lean into your grief and give yourself permission to move forward.

Leaning Into Grief Mantra:

Be Kind.

Be Loving.

Be Present.

Now I want you to treat yourself as if you were sitting with your best friend and comforting her. Would you get her a cup of hot tea? Would you offer her a cozy blanket? A box of soft tissues to dry her tears? Whatever nurturing gestures you would offer your best friend, offer these to yourself.

If you feel ready to lean into your grief, then let's make an appointment with your grief.

You have named your pain, so let's get to know your grief better. In detail, describe your grief. How big is it? What color is it? Write down any and all details.

_____

_____

_____

_____

_____

_____

_____

_____

_____

_____

_____

_____

_____

_____

_____

_____

_____

_____

Name your grief:

_____

_____

_____

_____

Take a moment and go get your hot tea, cozy blanket, and soft tissues. Next, find a safe, quiet place to sit with your mother's guide or your favorite journal. Once you have settled in, invite grief to come and sit with you.

Open your journal or write in your mother's guide book. Letter to grief: Write to grief and address your letter by grief's name. Let grief know what you are feeling. Let grief know everything about what you are experiencing including the pain, anger, and frustration. Lean into your grief.

DEAR _____ ,
(grief's name)

_____

_____

_____

_____

_____

_____

_____

_____

_____

_____

_____

_____

_____

_____

_____

_____

_____

_____

_____

_____

_____

_____

_____

_____

_____

_____

_____

Take a moment to comfort yourself. Sit and dry your tears, sip your hot tea, and wrap that cozy blanket around you. Do whatever feels like comfort to you.

You can sit with your grief whenever you choose to lean into it. You don't have to come up with any specific rules to sit with grief. With that in mind, remember that "what you resist will persist." It's essential to lean into grief rather than run away from it. I have learned that you cannot outrun grief. However, you can invite grief in, then let it know when it's time to leave. When you ask grief to leave, make sure you give thanks. It will leave you in a state of gratitude. Simply say, "Grief (*your grief's name*), thank you for listening; it's time for you to go now. See ya next time."

5

The Journey
to Understanding

Cycling in and out of grief is part of the mother guide autism journey. Yes, it is a journey, but how we live our lives on this journey is truly up to us.

I have used the word "journey" often in this book, because in my experience, understanding is a journey. Most journeys have many twists and turns. On my journey, I never really knew what to expect, but I did know I would eventually be okay.

I refer to my experience as an "autism journey." Although I began making decisions for Joseph as an infant, as time went on, I became a guide, and I continue to be his guide through life. I know that I will not punch a time card one day when I retire or hang up my mother's guide tennis shoes. I will continue to put on a brand-new pair of tennis shoes when this pair becomes worn out. I will keep guiding my son.

A journey can involve traveling a physical distance or traversing an emotional one. Some journeys last only a short while and others persist for a lifetime. This idea describes my past 29 years as Joseph's mother guide. Together, we have traveled from one place to another through time. There have been times of despair and times of joy during our journey. Joseph has his own ideas and goals for his life, and I have had my own personal goals and expectations along the way. Some of them were met, some were not, and some even exceeded my expectations.

I had the honor of being Joseph's teacher when he was a freshman in high school. The program that I was managing at the time was a life skills program. This was all part of a school reform that our district had adopted for every student enrolled in grades 9 through 12. My job was to prepare all freshmen with a six-year educational plan: four years of high school, plus a vision for two years post-secondary school.

As part of the Keystone curriculum, each week we had what we called a Fun Friday for all students who completed their assignments and stayed within our classroom discipline and other guidelines. One of the requirements was for each student to write in their journal on a specific topic. The goals were to improve content writing and for me to get to know each student.

I will never forget reading my son's first journal entry of the semester. This was a moment when my expectations were exceeded. I do not remember what the topic was, but I remember realizing after reading it that Joseph knew who he was. While I thought I knew him better than he knew himself, I was dead wrong. He understood the world much better than I did at his ripe old age of 14. Did he struggle with expressive language? Absolutely! However, his expressive writing was on point, and the words he chose were magical.

At that moment I knew he was going to be okay. Tears of relief and joy ran down my face as I re-read my son's words. It was as if I had found a key to a treasure chest of riches, giving me a deep understanding of my son. I felt like I had met him all over again. No one could ever take this moment from me. I just sat in the middle of the treasure chest with pure joy in my heart.

I moved on from that moment to promise myself that I needed to change how I viewed my son. Clearly, I was not understanding how his brain processed information. He had difficulty expressing himself verbally, but not through writing.

The lesson for me was that although I didn't have all the answers, neither did anyone else. Joseph is a unique individual with gifts; however, he struggles managing what society expects from him. As his mother guide, the struggle for me was how to navigate my son's uniqueness, gifts, and social quirkiness into an independent happy man.

I knew then that the road ahead would continue to be challenging for both of us. As with many days on my journey, the struggles often led to stressful moments that drained my spirit. I was not only trying to find my own way, but I was also searching for any signs of hope to keep guiding my son.

Along the journey, I found many different methods that gave me relief from the gray, dark days. I came across daily mantras, but, at first, I really didn't understand how to use them. I had always been a fan of inspirational quotes, so I thought I would find out more about mantras. This was a game changer for me – a simple way to apply the feelings of hope and inspiration to my daily life.

A mantra is a sound, word, or phrase that is repeated often, by someone who is praying or meditating, to express basic beliefs.

For our purposes, let's stick to personal mantras. A personal mantra is an affirmation to motivate and inspire you to be your best self. It's typically a positive phrase or statement that you use to affirm the way you want to live your life. The true value of a mantra comes when it is audible, visible, or in your thoughts.

Mantras have been utilized around the world for thousands of years. People use personal mantras to help them retrain their thoughts to focus on positive outcomes in order to reach their goals or transform the way they want to live their lives. Personal mantras can inspire you to achieve your greatest potential.

A mantra is intended to use your thoughts as a guide. It can help center your mind. By repeating your mantra out loud or silently within your own mind, you can guide your thoughts to the right frame of mind to achieve your goal or task. For example, before speaking publicly, you might say, "I am strong and I can do this" or "I believe in me."

Here are some examples of personal mantras that I have found helpful, from famous people.

> *"I am only one, but I am still one. I cannot do everything, but still, I can do something."*
> – Helen Keller

> *"Life shrinks or expands in proportion to one's courage."* – Anaïs Nin

> *"Do what you can, with what you have, where you are."* – Theodore Roosevelt

Someone else's quotes can be powerful personal mantras. If you would prefer to create your own personal mantra, then here are some steps you can take to help you.

Step 1: Take some time to sit in quiet and think about what you want your personal mantra to be.

Step 2: After you have decided upon your philosophy, find a quote by someone else or create your own quote that represents that philosophy. Usually, a short, powerful statement is best.

Step 3: If you are coming up empty, remember you can borrow someone else's quote until your own comes through to you.

Step 4: Once you have decided on your personal mantra, write it down and read it frequently. Setting some time aside each day to truly absorb your mantra is the best way for it to become part of who you are and how you live your life. Use it as a reminder to stay true to what you feel inside. Use it whenever you start to doubt yourself, when you wonder if you are capable of getting through your day, or when you just want to keep your life heading in a positive direction.

Here is one of the mantras I created not that long ago that I still pull out to use on days I need a loving affirmation: I am well, I am safe, I am grateful, I am. This helps me stay centered when I can feel negative thoughts and feelings creeping in.

Remember you can have more than one mantra, and you can also change a mantra any time to make it resonate with you. I strongly suggest writing your mantra down and putting it where you can see it often throughout your day.

My loving, healing mantra is:

_____

_____

_____

_____

_____

_____

_____

_____

6

Accepting That It's Okay to Not Be Okay

Now that you have a personal mantra, let's move forward with acceptance. One of my most powerful ahas was that maybe I could be happy and become okay with not being okay.

I heard a mother, who was well into her eighties, talk about how she was still not over the death of her daughter many years earlier. I listened as she spoke about living a life with adventure and joy after this devastating loss, and I applied it to myself. I realized then that I too was working hard to get over certain losses in my life, and that autism was one of them.

I asked myself, "What if I'm never okay with Joseph living with ASD?" At that moment I felt lighter. I realized that it's okay not to be okay with certain losses in life. That doesn't mean that I can't feel joy, laugh, or pursue my own dreams. All it means is that I can continue to struggle by putting all my energy into getting over it, or I can accept that this is what it is. Although I don't like it, I can be okay with it.

In Chapter 4, I discussed the five stages of grief; acceptance is the last stage of grief. I truly didn't understand that accepting my son's diagnosis didn't mean that I had to be happy about it. Grief isn't linear, and acceptance most definitely is not linear either.

Accepting that it's okay to not be okay with my son living with ASD simply means that I am no longer searching for a cure for my own heart. I often thought that if I kept working on my grief, one day I would wake up and feel just as I did before autism came into my life. Living with being okay with not being okay is simply living in the present moment and finding that, even on the hardest days, all is well.

Acceptance is all about processing our own goals and expectations after receiving the diagnosis of Autism Spectrum Disorder. This is part of the journey. Just as my son has evolved through many therapies, modifications, patience, problem-solving, and love, I have too.

There is no one secret recipe for acceptance. If I were to write one, though, I would begin with my own personal heart. Mother guides are always the team captains, even as the team players change. One player who will always be part of your team is your child. How we lead our team is up to what type of captain we decide to be. I fully understand the all-consuming pull to find answers that can help our children in any way we can. This pull can be overwhelming, and all mother guides need help with the how.

One essential component of any secret recipe of acceptance is doing your own work while you seek out resources for your child. You have learned by now that I am an advocate of hope and inspiration. Without these ingredients in your recipe, it will fail. I believe that there is always hope. Hold on to whatever hope you can find each day. Go back to the List of Hope exercise in Chapter 4 to help you feel hopeful when needed.

How mother guides perceive the diagnosis of our children is critical in how our children perceive their own lives on this journey. It's an evolutionary process, moving from one destination to another. One important ingredient I have found to be helpful in accepting the diagnosis of ASD is to let go of all negative beliefs and expectations. Set reasonable goals that don't feel too big, and live your life through a lens that is authentic, that is you. You are still allowed to have your own dreams.

Depending on where you are on your journey, you may not be ready to discuss your own personal dreams. You may still be deep in grief and pain, or just trying to take the first baby step forward on your autism journey. That is perfect. Meet your heart where it is at this moment.

Begin with putting small pieces of energy into taking tiny steps toward rediscovering joy. We all have joy deep in our hearts.

Our joy is still in our hearts, just as the sun is still in the sky when it is covered by clouds. We just have to be patient, and let those dark clouds of pain slowly dissolve. This is the work we are doing together throughout this book. Write down what you are okay with not being okay with today.

I am okay with not being okay with:

_____

_____

_____

_____

_____

_____

Now embrace the peace that comes with the statement that you wrote down. You are okay. Your child is okay. Your life is okay.

Take a breath. You can find joy in your life, although a dark cloud has temporarily taken your heart. The first thing I often say to any mother who is in that dark place is, "You are going to be okay." If you don't know anything else in those dark moments, know that you will not live in the darkness forever. Light, joy, and happiness will come through to you.

Accepting that your child is going to have challenges is a challenge itself. I know I went out to prove that my son was not going be left behind in this life. Certainly, there are pros and cons to this fighting spirit. One pro is that nothing can get in your way, and you will do whatever it takes to find answers for your child. The con is that you can miss living if you go down this rabbit hole too deep. I know I did.

I had no awareness that I was still living and breathing, as I sought answers and applied what I learned 24/7. I have recently gone back and looked through photo albums of Joseph's birthdays, holidays, and moments that appear on the surface to be filled with joy. But deep down, what I was feeling was a sense of being overwhelmed and a deep sadness any time I thought someone was judging Joseph or me.

I battled constantly to enjoy our time together. I lived many moments in fear, anger, and resentment. I was always planning my next move to find solutions. Living in this mode is exhausting – mentally, physically, and spiritually.

I don't like accepting things that I do not want in my life. I go right into fight mode and try to change what is, even when I know intellectually how it's going to be. I've been told that being a fighter when dealing with life's challenges is a positive character trait. As I get older, I still believe that it is, but I also have learned that I can be a fighter and still enjoy life. It's a paradox, but true.

I used to tell my students that we don't always have a choice over what happens to us, but we do have a choice over how we handle it.

My overarching life lesson is acceptance and finally letting go. I have learned that letting go is not giving up. I can continue to problem-solve life tsunamis without running against the wind.

At first, accepting Joseph's diagnosis was not in my thoughts. My heart was broken and I dug in my heels. I never considered taking a look at how I personally was processing my son's life-long, uphill diagnosis.

I truly believe that if I could have managed the emotional damage that I faced, our autism journey would still have been a climb, but a climb with more love and understanding. I would have been able to enjoy more of my life rather than swimming against the current.

Joseph used the metaphor of a river to explain how he let go of his own stressful times. He thought that it made more sense to flow with the current, rather than going against the flow.

My son is deeply profound. He is now flowing with the current of his life, and I try to remember to flow with mine. We both know that life tsunamis suck, and "it is what it is," so why not flow with grace?

I now know that I have a choice. I can choose to remain in fear and anger, or I can choose to let go and flow with life.

The question is how to let go and get to acceptance?

Here are 3 additional easy steps to take if you are swimming against the current. Try them. They work for me.

Step 1: Become aware that you are fighting what is. I practice noticing when I am deep with my head underwater and not willing to look up. This is when I am angry and dealing with a situation in my life that makes no sense. I get over the shock and then I move into anger. Anger is part of the grieving process to finally move into acceptance. I may rant and rave for a few days and then I realize that I have a choice to flow and let go. As I have this realization, I move on.

Step 2: Create and use a visual mantra to get out of the cycle of swimming against the current. I take a breath and can quickly see myself flowing with the current and enjoying the view with a big smile on my face. As I do this, I can feel the stress release. Although I do not have all the answers, I know that I will receive them. I always do.

Step 3: Go back to step 2 when you need it. I practice this and it works.

7

The Crazy
Monkeys of Fear

Do I still have moments when I worry about Joseph? You bet! I sometimes catch myself wondering if he will be able to manage his own life. When I begin to worry, all I have to do is pick up the phone and ask him how he's doing. Most of the time he says, "I'm not sure, but I love my life." That's enough for me. To hear my son assure me that he is happy, no matter what I perceive, is enough for me.

Although I have mostly good days now, and I know my son is happy, I still worry about what I call "crazy monkeys." Crazy monkeys are fear: one of the biggest energy suckers that a mother guide battles each and every day.

I first introduced this idea in one of my blogs titled The 3 Big Energy Suckers. Once we have received the diagnosis of autism, fear is ongoing, as we dare to peek into our child's future. There's hardly anything we don't worry about and fear: what will happen if…what will he do if…what if…what if?

As soon as I was brave enough to look forward to my son's new projected future, I felt only fear. I didn't want my son to suffer and to be living alone without me one day. I feared he would be living a life under the care of someone who didn't love or want him. What will happen to my son when I am gone?

I frequently told myself, "You cannot die until Joseph's future is taken care of." That was a fact, a truth for me. I really didn't have any emotion attached to that thought. It just was, and then I moved on to my next task of the day.

I now believe, looking back to that time, that making that statement was my numbing way to deal with fear. The truth is, I had no control of whether our future would work out as I planned it. I literally was doing all I could to just survive. I carried the fear with me each and every day.

Carrying my fear felt like lugging a bag of rocks on my back. Even with this heavy load, I expected myself to live as if I wasn't weighed down. I got used to dragging fear around with me. I rarely paid any attention to it, or how the stress of each day slowly caused my body to become weaker. I was oblivious to my exhaustion. Sure, I was tired, but so was every other mom I knew.

As Joseph got older, I became more certain that one day he would be able to live independently. I wasn't sure when, but I could see that he would. I knew this was a good thing, but I still felt some huge regrets. I wished that I could have known that he would be able to care for himself when he was first diagnosed. I was so focused on finding therapies that I missed some of the precious moments along the way.

Yes, it's understandable that I would be spending my energy on finding ways to help my son, but what if I could have done this without the huge energy sucker called fear? If I would have had the tools to manage my fear, perhaps I would have been a bit more present.

Fear is an inherent part of the autism journey. When I think about what fear really means, it gives me insight as to why any mother guide would carry it around each day. It's a belief that something terrible will happen; it's an emotion that scares and intimidates us.

To live in fear is exhausting. Ask yourself this question: If I could remove fear, how would I live my life differently?

_____

_____

_____

_____

_____

_____

_____

_____

_____

_____

If I could remove fear, how would I view my child and their future?

_____

_____

_____

_____

_____

_____

_____

_____

_____

_____

My hunch is that you will feel lighter living in the possibility that fear can't knock you down.

During most of the days I was living in deep fear, my intuition was whispering to me. All the negative thoughts flooded into my mind. My inner voice or intuition countered back, saying, "All is well, all will be well." Love for my son would then fill me up as I heard the whispers of hope, but as soon as the dim inner voice left, once again, I was completely filled with fear.

―――――

Crush the Crazy Monkeys of Fear with this mindful fear release exercise:

This exercise is simple. You will need a peaceful space, something to write in, such as a journal or this book. A pen or pencil to write your thought release answer. Maybe a tissue. Why? As I have worked through my pain and fears, I have found that when I hit a piece of inner truth, I either experience it through tears or goosebumps.

This is perfectly normal. Your body has a compass and knows the direction of truth. You may have noticed this working through the previous chapters.

I have had many clients who have feared doing this inner work because it is difficult to face the truth. Truth can hurt, but it also sets you free. The question to answer before moving on is, "Do you want to keep living in constant fear, or do you want to move through the fear?" I know this seems like an obvious question, but most inner work is obvious, as well as super scary.

Trust me. I have spent most of my life distracting myself in every way I could to avoid feeling what I feared the most. I am an expert at distracting myself from my feelings. This has led me to a lifelong illness and a compromised immune system, but now I seldom am ill. I believe my body continues to recover from years of living in fear. I now feel stronger and happier living in my own truth, whether it is good or ugly.

If you are ready to move through your fearful crazy monkey thoughts, here we go. If you are not ready, go do something kind for yourself. The day will come when you are ready. All is well.

As a reminder, all you need for this exercise is a peaceful space, something to write with, and a journal (or you can write your answers in this book).

Step 1:   Notice the beauty in your peaceful space. Look around and begin to feel each breath of peace.

Step 2:   Take three deep breaths in a row. When you breathe in, say the word "allow." When you exhale, say the word "surrender." You will notice the tension that you carry in your body letting go. During this exercise, when you begin to feel the tension returning, stop and take these three breaths in a row again to return to feeling calmer and more at peace. If you have fearful crazy monkey thoughts, picture these thoughts on a cloud. Visualize the cloud drifting away. Now go back to your breath. Each fearful thought will drift a way with each breath.

Step 3:   Ask this question to yourself out loud: "Without fear, how would I live my life?" Imagine life with no fear. You may need a few minutes to feel what it would be like without fear. Take your time. Imagine no fear. You can go back to your original answers that you wrote earlier in this chapter. Spend time living in this space as you imagine what your daily life might be like.

Step 4:   Describe what your life is like living without fear. Nothing has changed in your life, other than fear does not exist. This is where you take your answer and elaborate on the possibility. Begin at the very beginning of your day and write every detail here until you come to a peaceful stopping point.

_____

_____

_____

_____

_____

_____

_____

_____

_____

_____

_____

_____

_____

_____

_____

_____

_____

_____

Step 5: Read what you wrote. Now re-read what you wrote
out loud. Notice the shift you are feeling in your
body. My hunch is that you are feeling lighter.
The clouds are beginning to break up. The light is
beginning to peek through. Those dark clouds that
you have been seeing are dissipating. Just notice
how you feel. That's it.

Repeat this exercise as many times as you need to release your fearful crazy monkeys. Your thoughts are just thoughts. Your fearful thoughts are not real. Breathe deeply, and use your mantra that you created earlier to offer support as you crush the crazy monkeys and return to your peaceful space in your mind. The small steps you are taking throughout this book are brave and courageous.

You are allowing the light back in. This feeling of possibility and light is opening up the joy that you do have in your heart. This is the beginning of moving slowly, to living your life in this moment. All is well. Your energy will begin to return as you continue to give yourself permission to heal your mother's heart.

8

Living Life
as a Superhero

*"We all have the capacity to be a superhero.
In order to become one, you just have to
find your unique power or ability and exploit
it for the greater good. The cape and mask
are optional accessories, but a kind heart
is essential."*

- Robert Clancy

What I know for sure is that when I became a mother I transformed into a superhero. Instantly my senses heightened. Any pain I had was placed on the back burner. I could leap tall buildings with a single bound. My strength was beyond what I could comprehend. Fly? No problem. All it took was holding my son for the very first time.

Did you ever feel like a superhero?
Journal about that feeling. Write every detail.

What is your secret power as a superhero?

_____

_____

_____

_____

_____

_____

_____

_____

_____

All the powers I have now got me through these past almost 30 years. If you are wondering if you lose your powers once your children are grown, the answer is NO! The only difference now is that I am a bit wiser. I have learned how to conserve and use my powers at the right times.

What I didn't know as a novice superhero mom was that even superheroes become dim and exhausted. I was able to go for long periods of time with little to no sleep, not even brushing my teeth until late afternoon or evening. I could hold my bladder like a champ and subsist on very little nourishment throughout the day. I mostly ate what was left on my son's plate.

This was all doable. What wasn't doable was what I carried and held on the inside. My physical fatigue was exhausting. I now know that what truly drained my superhero powers was the deep pain of wanting to protect my son from anything or anyone who crossed his path with negative intentions. The problem was that I didn't know exactly how to protect him from whatever I envisioned as his threat or when it was going to show up.

Each morning when I dropped Joseph off at elementary school, I had a pit in my stomach as I watched him walk into the building. I held tight to a little notebook into which I wrote morning and evening to prepare his teacher for any triggers that could upset Joseph and disrupt his transitions throughout the day. In those days we didn't have cell phones or email to communicate, so I requested a notebook of communication with his teachers.

At the end of each school day, I anxiously awaited the return of the precious notebook with the teacher's accounting of my son's day. I still treasure those "survival notebooks" and the knowledge that I received about my son. Without them, I wouldn't have known anything about what happened each day, because, at that time, Joseph was not yet able to answer my questions.

Here is an entry from his kindergarten "survival notebook."

9 / 26 / 1997 — *Morning note to his teacher from me*

> *Very excited to get another Happy Gram.*
> *I was thinking about that hyperlexic information…It talks a lot about socialization. I was wondering how to address them. I thought if we made a list of some of the things Joseph didn't get (e.g., turning, talking, playing what other children want to play), then take one issue at a time. Maybe use some of the approaches they suggest. I'm not done digging for more help. What do you think?*
>
> P.S. *Also, classroom management issues for Joseph.*

9 / 26 / 1997 — *Afternoon note from his teacher*

> *Hi! We had another good day! We made applesauce, had an apple taste test, and apple printed. It was a fun day! Making lists sounds like a good idea. I will put some ideas together this weekend and you do the same. I know social story writing really seems to help!! Have a great weekend! Do something special for "our boy." He's earned it!*
>
> P.S. *He really enjoyed showing his animals for show and tell. He loves elephants!!*

This is one brief example of daily communication with Joseph's classroom teacher. Each day, these entries brought a wealth of opportunity to discover how to help my son move forward with love and patience.

As Joseph got a little older, he was able to tell me bits and pieces about his school days. By the time he was in fourth grade, he was able to communicate well enough that I no longer needed to use the notebook. I was also able to volunteer in the classroom, where I became acquainted with his classmates and the other parents who were involved in school activities. Even with the notebook, I still had that pit in my stomach most of the time, as I watched the painful reality that my son was clueless about how to interact with the other children.

I invited every single boy in his classroom to come to a sleepover birthday party. I felt that if we had his classmates over to our home, a familiar environment for Joseph, that he would be more comfortable and just maybe find a playmate. Well, it went pretty well other than none of us getting any sleep and having a rather large mess to clean up in the morning. It absolutely would have been worth it if Joseph had a good time and found a friend. He did have a good time, but he didn't end up with a friend. The point I am trying to make is that no matter what the occasion, I was living in superhero mode.

What superhero moves have you made for your child?

_____

_____

_____

_____

_____

_____

_____

_____

Living life as a superhero is admirable and exhausting. Each day that went by, I unknowingly carried this pit of despair around with me. Although I felt the exhaustion early on, I used every ounce of my will to keep moving forward. I never considered slowing down to catch my breath. I didn't know that even superheroes need to refuel and rest to re-energize their powers.

During this time, I started a support group for our rural area to share resources with teachers and parents. My group gave us all a safe space to talk about what we were experiencing and to give each other hope for our children. I facilitated this group for two years. Each month I rented and picked up folding chairs, stopped by our local bakery for snacks, and made copies of any resources that I could find to share. I invited guest speakers, ran ads in our local paper, and showed up with the anticipation of running an inspiring meeting.

At first the meetings were full of eager parents looking for answers. After a while, our numbers began to dwindle, and so did I. I remember thinking often how tired I felt; still, I believed that this was just how it was supposed to be. I never considered the option that I didn't have to live my life feeling exhausted. I had no idea that I had a choice.

How do you know when your superhero powers are fading and need to be recharged? What happens?

_____

_____

_____

_____

_____

_____

_____

_____

If I would have known that it was possible to refuel my energy, I might not have missed so many days of joy. I truly believe that my health might not have failed. The fact is that I didn't know and that's okay. As Maya Angelou has said, "Do the best you can until you know better. Then when you know better, do better." You don't know what you don't know. This is why I feel so strongly about sharing my experience with you.

Even if you find yourself resisting the tools that follow to help you refuel your superhero powers, you can come back to them when you are ready to ease your stress. A simple question to ask yourself is, "How do I feel?" You may instantly answer the obvious: tired, exhausted, fed up, meh, blah, sick of it, etc. Whatever your initial answer is, these practices can slow things down.

Once again, if you are not ready to dive into refueling your superhero mother guide powers, no problem. Come back to these practices whenever you are ready. For now, go do something kind for yourself that will recharge you too.

Superhero refueling practices:

Find a peaceful or safe space, something to write with, and begin with three deep breaths.

Answer this question: How do I feel?

_____

_____

_____

_____

_____

_____

_____

You may have answered with the obvious examples that I gave earlier, but now take those three deep breaths again, and answer the same question. This time we are going to add data to your feelings.

How do I feel?

_____

_____

_____

_____

_____

_____

Is there a feeling that takes over? My hunch is that exhaustion is the main feeling that comes through, because it is a common feeling amongst superhero mother guides. If you have a different one, please use whatever is living inside of you. Notice whatever you are feeling.

What is causing me to feel this way? Why are you exhausted? Or sad or anxious? Give reasons that you think are contributing to your feelings. Don't hold back. Put it all down here.

_____

_____

_____

_____

_____

_____

What is the main reason you feel this way? The cause. The why.

_____

_____

_____

_____

_____

_____

_____

_____

_____

_____

_____

_____

I will use exhaustion as your main feeling, as an example of how to work through this practice.

Now that you know what you're feeling frequently and why, let's shift from the feeling of exhaustion to feeling more rested and energized.

Take those three big beautiful breaths once again, and imagine a day when you are filled with energy.

How would you live a day filled with energy? Give details about your energized day from when you wake up until you rest your head down on the pillow at the end of your day.

Don't hold back. Write down everything that comes up for you. Anything is possible. Tune into your senses.

Begin with "I wake up, and I hear, see, smell, feel..."

Now I want you to go back and read what your energized day was like, and notice how you feel when you are reading your day back to yourself.

What are you feeling as you finish reading about the day that you are imagining?

_____

_____

_____

_____

_____

_____

_____

_____

Does this day filled with energy feel impossible? I want you to know that I truly believe that you can have the day you are dreaming about.

When I began the support group, my intention was to give others resources and support. What I didn't realize is that I needed the support too, maybe more than anyone who attended. I was terrible at asking for help. I had the belief that I didn't need it, and during those days when I really needed support, I kept it to myself.

I would like to take a moment and thank my parents, in-laws, extended family, and friends for the love and support that they gave me during those times. The truth is that I needed more than I even knew I needed. I felt like a weak person to ask for more support than what I was already getting. I felt deep guilt, like I wasn't a good mother if I asked for more help.

I learned years later that asking for help is in fact a prayer. Michael Beckwith discussed this on Oprah's Super Soul Sunday program. He explained that if you use the word "HELP" as an acronym for Hello Eternal Loving Presence, it can become a beautiful prayer. I now use it as one of my mantras.

As you are asking for help from this deep place inside your heart, you are asking with grace. Asking for help as a prayer is grace, and help and support will come to you. I know it has come to me. To this day, I use this prayer and as always, my prayer is answered in a way I could not have imagined.

Refueling energy works differently for everyone. When your fuel tank is low or close to empty, it feels impossible to move forward. You feel stuck. The thought of working on yourself to feel better can feel way too big. So, let's make it smaller. Let's take one tiny step at a time and begin refueling your superhero powers.

My tiny steps to refuel my superhero powers:

Let's go back to your day filled with energy.

As you finish reading your day filled with what you are imagining in your life, what is one tiny step you can take to move toward living this day?

_____

_____

_____

_____

_____

_____

Whatever your first step is, read it back to yourself. You might have answered: getting some sleep, enjoying a date night or girls' night out, reading a book, or taking a long, hot bath. You can change your answer until it feels truly doable.

For example, if your tiny first step is taking a walk, then take a deep breath and check in with yourself. Does this first step feel too big? If it does, then how can you make it smaller? Keep making your first tiny step smaller until it feels exciting inside of you. You will know when it feels good and not scary. It will feel like a step toward living a day that you crave.

If you need HELP, use your mantra of prayer and ask someone to help you. I know it might feel big, so ask for a smaller piece of support to get started. It does not matter how big or small your first tiny step is, as long as you are moving forward.

Now go do one small act of kindness for yourself.

Let Kindness Be Your Superpower Today!

9

Rocking Advocacy
with Kindness

I started advocating for Joseph on the day he was born, long before I knew he had a lifelong disability, and five years before I gave birth to my neurotypical son. Advocating is inherent in the mother guide superhero journey. It is part of each breath that I took once I became a mother.

From the moment we knew our lives were going to be different from being parents of a neurotypical child, my husband and I decided that we would do anything humanly possible to give Joseph a better life. I recall so many examples of when I advocated for Joseph that this one chapter could turn into a book all its own.

My roles as an advocate were different for each of my two children. I believe that these two types of parenting aren't all that different until they need to be different. Joseph needed me to be his advocate for everything. My second son needed me to be his advocate only in some situations. I realized the difference between how to advocate for a child who has a lifelong developmental disability and for a child who hits occasional bumps in the road. My neurotypical son needed a parent who advocated, but he also was advocating for himself early on, and later, even began to protect and advocate for his older brother. I now have both perspectives.

As soon as Joseph entered public education, I understood that he needed me to be his advocate from both a mother's and an educator's point of view. I had a real advantage as an educator who was very familiar with school policy, the teachers, and school administrators. This knowledge helped me navigate my strategies for my son each school year.

What I didn't realize was how pervasive every experience was going to be as my son's advocate. I had to learn the ins and outs of the law, each teacher's classroom management style, level of understanding and empathy, and school policies.

I quickly discovered that each decision I made had crucial short-term and long-term impacts on Joseph's experiences. However, no matter what I thought I knew, or whom I knew, major crises occurred that I didn't see coming. It really didn't matter whether I was advocating with a doctor, therapist, teacher, neighbor, or family member, because it was always the same process. Once I left the encounter, I often readdressed the situation to problem-solve how to get whatever it was Joseph needed. The challenge was always trying to stay on track to obtain the outcome I wanted for my son. As you advocate for your child, focus on the goal and use your mother's guidance, intuition, and passion as fuel to problem-solve and find a way to get there.

———

1. I usually started with a "why" of needing to meet with them. For example, when I had a conference with a classroom teacher who would be navigating most of Joseph's school days one year, I prepared a detailed explanation of what Joseph's needs were in order to be successful in his educational environment. I thought if I could support both the teacher and my son, then we had a pretty good chance of being successful.

2. Sometimes I needed to remind myself that whomever I was speaking with did not know much about either my son or autism. I had to be strategic in a way that kept the meeting positive and not scary.

3. I realized often that, although I gave it my best shot, some professionals didn't really comprehend what I was attempting to explain. Few conversations ended in a deep understanding of how to determine the least invasive path for my son. I knew at some point that frustration was going to be a part of the experience for both sides.

4. I tried hard to channel my anger and frustration as fuel to keep us all on a positive path toward finding resources. I tried to stay at least five steps ahead with possibilities of solutions. My support group was my outlet for my anger and frustration, and it kept me from losing my mind and temper with others. Support is essential.

5. I learned quickly that if my best efforts did not result in connecting, then I needed to go back to the drawing board. Sometimes I found a solution quickly; other times I did not.

6. Advocating was exhausting at times, but always worth the effort in the end.

7. Even though many people entered meetings in a defensive mode, I tried hard to stay in a zone of kindness that focused on the big picture – my son.

Joseph's early school days were surely challenging, but nothing like the later years.

When he started kindergarten, the big challenge was proving that he could be in a mainstream classroom with neurotypical learners. One suggestion was that Joseph spend a half-day in the mainstream and then the rest in a self-contained special education classroom. An administrator once also recommended that we ask our doctor for medication to help Joseph pay attention better.

I nodded and listened to all their suggestions, while knowing that my goal was for Joseph to be in a mainstream classroom environment full time and without medication. I knew my son, and I was certain that he would be able to succeed if he had a classroom teacher who would be willing to work with my child.

I reached out to the teacher that I knew would be our first "earth angel" to accept my son with open arms. I can remember having a feeling of relief when I knew that he would have a loving teacher. The moment was brief, and then I went back to work to solve our next obstacle. No matter what was before us, I knew that there was always a way. With constant problem-solving combined with a little luck and lots of love, we made the miracle of inclusion happen.

I believe that the mothers who I have interviewed for the **Mother's Guide Through Autism** podcast are some of the very best problem-solvers in the world, and they get very little credit. I have seen mothers step up so many times in order to create some of the world's top solutions for their children living on the autism spectrum. When they hit a wall that is blocking their child's future, they find a way to knock it down and help other parents with the same challenges. Mothers bring other parents and kids on the spectrum along to benefit from the successes and find answers. These women are not only problem-solving, but also making a difference that results in happy, productive lives for our children.

One of my main thoughts when I hit some of my own personal walls as my son's advocate was to consider that each teacher, administrator, or parent may have had negative experiences with other parents of children with disabilities. Maybe some simply did not have the knowledge to help my child. There were also some educators who did not want anything to do with my son. Why were they so fearful?

I began advocating at the end of each year before Joseph entered the next school year. Here we were, getting ready for third grade, and I had already figured out which classroom teacher was going to be the quarterback for Joseph's team of teachers. I was thrilled when one of my best friends was going to be my son's third grade classroom teacher.

This was the first year that teachers nominated students to be considered for the Gifted and Talented program. Joseph's teacher nominated him. He passed all the markers with flying colors except for one caveat – he also had an Individualized Educational Plan (IEP).

We went through steps to give Joseph the opportunity to be in the Gifted and Talented program. However, a board of administrators and teachers decided which children were accepted, and they declined Joseph. The administrator who oversaw the program erroneously believed that a special education student could not also be a gifted student.

I even showed this man Joseph's nonverbal IQ scores, which were in the genius range. I will never forget the look on his face. He glared at me as he reached out to take the folder from my hand. He never uttered a word. I walked out, determined not to be intimidated. If I had to, I would find another way.

What resulted was that Joseph's core teachers, including the Gifted and Talented teacher, all worked together. Joseph participated in all of the Gifted and Talented activities, although he was not officially in the program.

I volunteered and went on all the field trips, and Joseph did the same special projects as the other children in the program. I remember thinking that each child should be able to have the level of education that the children in this program were provided. This was a mission I would later address in my educational career.

The next step that my husband and I took was to become coaches for the Odyssey of the Mind, a program that teaches students how to develop and use their natural creativity to become problem-solvers. This was the first year that OM™ was offered to third graders. We went through the training and coached Joseph's team. We drew the theme for our competition called The Idiom Inspiration.

Idioms for a child on the spectrum are a challenging concept, but Joseph caught on very fast. He knew so many phrases, and loved "it's raining cats and dogs." For a literal mind, I imagined he thought it would literally rain cats and dogs!

So, although our son was rejected from inclusion in the Gifted and Talented program because he was a special education student, we managed to become parent coaches for a gifted and talented competition. The administrator who rejected him came to our competitions that spring. He glared at us, but never spoke to us. Deep down, I knew that we had proven that our son and others on the spectrum had the right to participate in any program they qualified for.

Years later, when I went back into education, and I was an administrator of the Career Academy program, this same man came up to me at a conference. Believe it or not, he apologized to me! He finally understood that students with autism did not have to live a life with limitations. They, like neurotypical kids, could live a life full of gifts, where anything was possible.

The heart of the matter is that I knew my son. I knew what his weaknesses were, because those were the focus of his diagnosis, educational plan, and what most of his life was about at that time. However, he also had gifts to offer the world.

My mother's heart would not allow someone else to define and limit what I knew my son was capable of. My heart is stronger than anyone else's when it comes to my children. It knows the way. It is scarred from being broken, but it has come back bigger and stronger from my life experiences. I have never met a mother who didn't have pieces of her heart broken on this autism journey. I believe that when you get to the heart of the matter, that is when you find the way. I have helped mother guides get to the heart of the matter and when they get to it, they also know the way.

I could have let my anger lead me in how I advocated for my son. However, I decided that to truly change how my son and other students on the spectrum would be taught, I needed to pave the road one day at a time. I shifted to changing the bigger picture of educating autistic students. I do believe we have come a long way from the late 1990s, and we still have a long way to go.

With that said, being your child's advocate is also draining and has many challenges. One of the main challenges for me was that I felt alone much of the time. I did have support from teachers and friends who truly tried to understand, and they did what they could to help us. But, at the end of the day, they had their own lives to live.

I felt alone especially when attending school functions. When I look back at myself as a 32-year-old mother of a special needs son, I felt so overwhelmed. I was at the beginning of my autism journey and had no idea how to navigate it.

I recognized that as different as my son was from his own peers, I was as different from mine. I despised the condescending looks of pity I got from the other mothers. I knew deep down inside that their intentions were not to make me feel bad about myself, but they did anyway. Although my main motivations were to be an essential part of Joseph's school environment and to help him navigate through every challenging situation, I also had to navigate my complicated feelings.

Honorable advocates are people who aren't afraid to stick their necks out or be "lone wolves." They are sometimes ostracized. They might also be thanked later for their insights, courage, and forward-thinking views. They also lead by example and try to bring out the best in others by using words of encouragement.

I have heard the saying that if you can't be a part of the solution, then you are part of the problem. In other words, come to the table with solutions. I never took "no" for an answer. I continued to show up and I used my superhero powers to shield the dirty looks of judgment. I took the extra step to mentor others on how to become good advocates themselves.

No wonder I was so exhausted all the time. Yet, I would do it all over again. The only thing I would change is incorporating some of the self-help tools that I have learned over the past 30+ years.

One essential strategy I relied upon to navigate each surprise attack was kindness. No matter what, I looked my adversaries in their eyes and thanked them for whatever they threw at me. My thoughts may not have been kind, but I always left each meeting with a heartfelt "thank you." Advocating with kindness is the proactive way to lead the path for your child.

Here are helpful tips that I have learned through my mother guide journey.

Tips to advocate with kindness:

An advocate is a person who stands up for a person, cause, or philosophy. An advocate defends and supports the person they care about.

Kindness is an action, a way of showing love, affection, and care for another person. Kindness is often given without expectation of being reciprocated.

When I put these two definitions together, it empowers me to advocate through speaking, writing, teaching, defending, and supporting others. I do this through acts of generosity, concern, and consideration for others, especially those on the autism spectrum.

Putting this advocacy with kindness into action steps:

1. Build your support team. Yes, being an honorable advocate may set you apart as the "lone wolf," but it doesn't mean that you have to be. Build your own "wolf pack" by making connections in your community. If there is a local support group for parents with kids on the autism spectrum, become an active member. If there isn't one, then maybe you can start one. I have found that once you take the first step, then other parents will follow, join, and help out. We all need support. We all need our own "wolf pack." Being a quarterback of your team is fueled by knowing you are making a difference. You can lead by following your heart.

2. Volunteer. When you volunteer, you get to know your child's teachers, school administrators, and other parents who are engaging with your child on a daily basis. Be as present and involved as you can be. It doesn't have to be

every day or even every week. The first step is to ask: How can I help? Where can I volunteer? Let your child's teacher know the times and days that you are available. It may be challenging to problem-solve volunteering, but just remember to begin small and go from there.

Many mother guides are single moms who work hard to support their children. I became a single mom in 2005 and it was tough. When you become part of a "wolf pack," ask for help. Remember that prayer: **Hello Eternal Loving Presence.**

3. Communicate. It is the glue for success in advocating with kindness. How you communicate, how often, and to whom are so essential. I always told my two sons that words are powerful. Have an open dialogue with your child's teachers, administrators, other parents, "wolf pack," and most importantly, your child.

Having clarity about your intentional outcome will guide your communication. Don't assume that others know what you and your child need. Once you are clear about what you need, then choose your words to create the best possible outcome. Practice what you want to say, and get feedback before entering a meeting, conference, or encounter.

Communication is a skill that takes practice. If you are taken by surprise, and the outcome is not what you had hoped for, then pause and go back to the drawing board to get what you need to be heard. This will get easier, and remember, if you leave a conversation feeling like you or the other person could have done a better job: know better, do better. This skill will be one of your best tools to advocate honorably and kindly.

4. Find resources to support your cause. Whenever I entered any meeting or conference, I always had resources in hand. You are the expert when it comes to your child. You know your child's needs better than anyone else on earth. There will be people who reject your resources, but most of the

time, they will welcome any strategies that you have to help your child thrive. If researching resources feels overwhelming, begin with the topic that your child needs the most at that moment. What will help your child move forward one tiny step at a time?

5. Advocate with kindness for yourself. I have found that this is the most difficult practice for many mother guides. Believe me, I rejected putting myself first in all areas of my life. My 32-year-old self would have snickered at this concept, but this is the golden ticket. I will elaborate more in a later chapter because I do believe that this could be the game changer for you to transform a lifelong disability from fear to joy and possibility. For now, let's go back to an earlier chapter and use your mantras and small acts of kindness for yourself. I will repeat this practice because it is essential in living with deeper purpose and joy.

As you move through these advocacy tips with kindness, remember that this is a journey. If you aren't ready to move through this exercise, then come back when you are ready. As always, go and give yourself love and kindness. Remember this is essential.

How will you advocate with kindness? Think about your next possible advocacy opportunity. How will you apply your advocacy kindness tips to this experience?

Outcome goal:

_____

_____

_____

_____

_____

_____

Who is on your support team?

_____

_____

_____

_____

_____

_____

How can you network or volunteer and with whom?

_____

_____

_____

_____

_____

_____

Communication strategies:

_____

_____

_____

_____

_____

_____

_____

_____

What resources have been found to support your goal?

_____

_____

_____

_____

_____

_____

What is your act of self-kindness as you are preparing?

_____

_____

_____

_____

_____

_____

_____

We will be on the mother guide journey our whole life. Although it will transform, once we become a mother guide, we are always a mother guide. To be an advocate is being a superhero to spread love, understanding, and kindness to make this world a world of inclusion for our children.

10

Always a
Mother Guide

There's nothing like Joseph's one-liners to make me ponder the truth that he speaks. Several years ago, I asked him what he thought my biggest life lesson was. He instantly answered, "You need to learn how to let go." Apparently, he has observed more about me than I have ever given him credit for on our journey together.

I knew that he was absolutely right! Yes, I did need to learn how to let things go. Joseph introduced me to Joseph Campbell, the American mythologist, writer, and lecturer, and his work from which I am now learning.

Here is one of Joseph Campbell's quotes that I want to share with you.

> *"We must let go of the life we have planned, so as to accept the one that is waiting for us."*

When I read this, I instantly thought of what my son had so wisely shared with me. Yes, I needed to let go so that I could live the life that I had with more joy and grace. I had struggled to let go of pretty much anything that didn't go my way.

I wanted to know more about "letting go" in terms of how to live my life more positively. I read books and articles on this subject and discovered when I held onto something, I was in fact "bargaining." Elisabeth Kubler-Ross, in her 1969 ground-breaking classic **On Death and Dying**, changed our thinking about the grief process. Today, her theory of the stages of grief is applied not only to bereavement, but is also relevant to any difficult adjustment process.[1] We all want to hold onto things, people, places, and life circumstances, because we don't want to lose them. We often hold on even longer when we get stuck in the bargaining stage.

---

[1] Kubler-Ross, Elisabeth. **On Death and Dying: What the Dying Have To Teach Doctors, Nurses, Clergy, & Their Own Families.** Routledge, 1969.

I can really relate to this idea of bargaining. I often bargained with God, praying that if he changed whatever I needed, then I would do X, Y, or Z. Sometimes, my prayers would be answered, and then I thought I better follow through on what I had promised, or I might get hit by lightning. Luckily, I usually did a pretty good job of keeping my promises to God.

When you bargain you may believe that the loss is "wrong" and then must be made "right." When I think of the loss I felt when Joseph was diagnosed, it definitely felt wrong. I know that I didn't plan on this, nor did I want to see my child suffer. I had a hard time accepting what life has dealt me. I do hold on, and I bargain when I'm not ready to let go.

What I have learned is that letting go is truly having faith, allowing life to flow, and becoming a person with a deeper understanding of self. When I catch myself getting stuck in bargaining, I can now practice "allowing" with grace.

I love this prayer:

> *God, grant me the Serenity to accept the things I cannot change, the Courage to change the things I can, and the Wisdom to know the difference.*

For parents of children with autism, letting go is essential. No, I didn't plan on having a child with a lifelong disability, but then I also didn't plan for life at 58 years old as it is today. I am a single empty-nester, a new business owner, a Type 1 diabetic, and loving every minute of "what is" on most days.

The difference now is that I have been able to shift how I perceive my life. My plans may not work out, but maybe the actuality of my life is better than what I had planned. Joseph is exactly who he needs to be. I couldn't see that for many years. Although I wanted a different life for him, his life has become his own.

When I was navigating teaching my son to be independent, I struggled constantly with how much freedom to give him. Most parents struggle with this when raising a teenager, but for me, balancing how much independence to give Joseph was really challenging. I knew he was capable of a great deal, but he had trouble knowing who he could trust and who was manipulating him. He naively trusted and believed everyone.

I know that I also was quite gullible as a young person, but I usually caught on quickly when someone was trying to persuade me to do something that was not in my best interest or that would have harmed me or others.

Joseph repeatedly let his young peers take advantage of his pure heart. I desperately wanted to follow him around and protect him, but I knew that at some point he would need to be able to navigate relationships on his own. Slowly, during his teenage years, I was able to stand back and observe and stay out of the less harmful encounters. I can recall so many examples of him being bullied, manipulated, and deceived during those years; I realized that he needed to learn lessons through these painful life experiences.

Wow! That was **REALLY** hard to do. When my son came to me with hurt feelings, I had to spend many hours explaining how else he might have navigated each situation differently. Just as I knew he needed to experience actually flying in an airplane to lose his associated fear, he needed to experience hurtful feelings to learn many of life's lessons. He learned that he loved to fly, and that some people in his life would hurt him because they weren't good people. It's challenging, to say the least, to teach life's lessons to someone whose greatest deficit is being socially challenged. I knew though that he would take each experience and file it away to apply to the next one.

Joseph slowly became socially literate through trial and error. He began with small life lessons, and he learned how to apply each one to the more potentially harmful outcomes relating to sex, drugs, and alcohol. I was close to each of these situations, and he did pretty well for the most part.

Joseph was extremely fearful of getting in trouble with the law and knew he didn't want to spend one hour in jail. He was very good about not drinking and driving. He saw someone he cared about get arrested, and through observation, he made every effort not to be handcuffed and taken into the police station.

The more experiences he had, the better he was able to navigate his own life. The best thing about learning from experience is that it doesn't have to happen directly to people on the spectrum. They can learn by watching what happens to others, whether it be in real life, a movie, or in any other way.

The bottom line is that we will make mistakes, and so will our children. Learning life's lessons in tiny steps works best, but when our kids jump ahead fast and make big mistakes, we need to be ready to use each experience as a deep teaching moment. Trust me, they will remember what happened, file it away, and learn from it.

Letting go of being a full-time advocate and hands-on parent navigating Joseph's life has been challenging. I was the expert captain of my son's ship, because that's what I was called to do. I didn't apply for this job or have any training for my mother guide position. I learned through experience, just as my son has done.

Much of what I learned was through observation, trial and error, research, and deep support. After struggles, we dusted ourselves off, and Joseph took small steps toward living an independent life. My love for my son has always been the motivating force that has kept me going through my dark, exhausting days.

I knew all along that I was a superhero, and my purpose was clear. I needed the tools that this book offers you, but I didn't have them then. I looked for any signs. Even when progress was minimal, nothing mattered as long as we were moving forward. Some days it felt like we took three steps forward and two steps back, but we always kept our goals in mind.

I have referred to my mother guide experience as a journey because it's the best way I can explain what my life as Joseph's mom has been for almost three decades. My experiences have brought me both twists and turns of unexpected pain, as well as unexpected joy. The emotions that I have experienced have not diminished; they all feel familiar as I continue to move forward with my son.

Each chapter you have read with my stories of pain, denial, acceptance, judgment, and discovery of joy and happiness is a cycle in the journey that I have experienced. Using the tools from each chapter can give you the resilience that you too will need on your journey. They are tools and practices to be used over and over again. My hunch is that you will reach for them on most days.

Although Joseph is thriving now, my journey hasn't ended yet. I am still parenting and staying close, while being very careful about giving him his freedom. Joseph lived with me at home until he was 29 years old. This gave me the extra time that I felt he and I both needed for him to transition into adulthood.

I accompanied him to open his first bank account, to buy his first car, to get his auto insurance, to pay taxes, to change his oil, to manage his cell phone and bills, and how to apply for and keep a job. I taught him that you don't quit a job until you have another one lined up. I recommended that he always give two weeks' notice. We both knew when he was ready to venture out on his own.

He met a lovely young lady online who lived a couple of hours away. She began coming to visit, and he went to visit her. When the time came, he made the decision to quit his job and move 126 miles away. He came home one evening after he completed his shift at the local radio station where he was working and told me he gave his two weeks' notice.

I was shocked that he quit, because I knew he didn't have another job. I knew he had saved some money, but I have to admit I was pretty upset. I kept my cool for a bit. I knew that if I got visibly upset, then he would get upset, and it would take a while to get to the important conversation that we needed to have. I asked him if he had another job, although I knew he didn't. He confirmed what I knew and said that he was applying online for jobs. He felt confident that he would have one soon and that he was very happy about moving.

Then I started to cry from sheer, deeply jumbled emotions, and he began to cry, and then we were both sobbing. I was crying because I was feeling sad, scared for him, and unsure that he was ready at that moment. He was crying because he was sad, sad for me, and also unsure.

Once we caught our breath, we hugged, and I knew for sure that I needed to step up and support his move. Did I believe it was too big for him? Yes. But I also knew this was how I raised my son: to believe in himself just as I had his whole life. I told him how proud I was of him, and I decided to support him as much as I could to make this decision a successful one.

How he got to this point was certainly not what I had planned for him, even though I knew that it was how he needed to proceed. He had to follow his own life path, not mine. This major step was extremely difficult for me. My crazy monkeys of fear took over once again. I feared that if Joseph didn't follow a more traditional plan, that he could, at worst, become homeless one day. I also didn't want him to be lost and sad because he didn't have me to give him the direction and support he needed. Thank goodness I had the tools to work through my deep fears, and I used them.

I helped Joseph rent a U-Haul, and he, a roommate, and his girlfriend moved his bedroom furniture and belongings out of my house on February 6, 2021. He called me when he arrived at his new home to let me know he was okay. His voice was full of hope and joy. He was so happy. I knew at that moment that all the years of being his mother guide were being realized. The foundations that I had laid for Joseph were now supporting him. Was my job as a mother guide finished?

No way! I now guide him during our frequent phone conversations and when he comes home to visit. Our relationship is stronger than ever. I miss him so much, and I keep reminding myself how happy my son is. His happiness was my goal from the day he was born. All I ever wanted was for my children to be happy. How they got there was up to them.

My mantra during this time was:
It's okay. Joseph is happy. All is well.

He paved his own path, and, frankly, I am amazed. As I have had to let go of my plan, I can clearly see that his plan is smoother and happier than any I could have ever paved myself.

Take a moment and list as many plans that you made for your child that have changed. Examples might be that a therapy you desperately wanted for your child had to be delayed, and, as a result of having to wait, you were able to find the right therapist.

———

List five big or small changes.

1.

2.

3.

4.

5.

Which of these changes ended up being for the better?

1.

2.

3.

4.

5.

My hunch is that most turned out better than the original plans. I will never be jumping up and down about my son being autistic, and that's okay. I am jumping up and down about who he has become today. I accept his beauty unconditionally.

I know that I will have to continue practicing letting go of my own plans and to accept the life that I was meant to live. How?

Here is a simple practice that I often use to live with what is, and with the life that is waiting for me.

Practice letting go with tiny steps of change:

What do you need to let go of at this moment?

_____

_____

_____

_____

_____

Are you stuck in bargaining?
If yes, write about what is keeping you stuck.

_____

_____

_____

_____

_____

_____

_____

Are you holding onto something that you know cannot change?
Why?

_____

_____

_____

_____

_____

_____

_____

_____

_____

_____

_____

_____

_____

What can you change? Choose something small for now. Check in and make sure it feels like you can presently take action to change it.

_____

_____

_____

_____

_____

_____

_____

What is one tiny step that you can take today toward your doable change?

_____

_____

_____

_____

_____

_____

_____

_____

_____

_____

Stay focused on your tiny step of change. Once you have completed your tiny step of change, celebrate with one small act of self-kindness.

My small self-kindness act today is:

_____

_____

_____

_____

_____

_____

Remember that once a mother guide, always a mother guide. Move forward in grace and self-kindness. Although this can often be challenging, you can do it.

11

Moving Forward with Self-Compassion

Learning how to practice self-compassion is one of the biggest challenges of being a mother guide. Most moms are brilliant at nurturing everyone but themselves.

I am one of those moms who struggled hard to learn how to nurture herself. What I mean by "nurture" is to go deeper than scheduling a massage or a manicure, although I strongly support both of those self-care practices. Self-compassion is deep and more comprehensive work.

When I was a teacher in the public school system, I taught the whole child: mind, body, and spirit. Likewise, self-compassion includes my whole self: mind, body, and spirit.

My personal definition of self-compassion is to nurture myself whenever I need it, each and every day. It includes showing myself kindness and offering myself understanding and forgiveness, even when I don't show up. Most of all, it is paying attention to what my spirit is craving and feeding it.

Self-compassion is the most difficult of all the tools I use when I coach mother guides. I think I understand why. My hunch is that your crazy monkeys of fear are taking over even as you read these words. I get it, because I've been there. It's just much easier to spend whatever precious time you have on others. However, I promise you if you can incorporate this concept into your daily life, you will be a better guide to your child, and you'll be a happier person.

I want to be very clear when I say that this could be the most challenging practice I am suggesting to incorporate in your daily life, because as I have stated, most moms simply don't know how to nurture themselves. I was great at executing the hundreds of tasks that I got checked off each day, while my energy, spirit, and joy were sucked dry.

For now, just take a breath and keep reading. I want to give you more information about what self-compassion is and tiny steps to take to incorporate it daily.

Self-compassion encompasses all of the key skills or characteristics of building resilience. I have discovered that as I gradually learned how to take care of myself, I have become more resilient.

Most mother guides encounter a great deal of resistance when they attempt to put themselves first because family, friends, a career, and their child on the spectrum all demand attention. I used to have a sarcastic smile on my face when I heard anyone speaking about caring for themselves. I thought, "Yeah right, like that's gonna happen."

At first, I didn't even give this idea a chance to evolve into a reality. I shut it down before I could ever consider the thought of filling myself up before attending to anyone else. If you are like me and you are shutting down, take a breath and just hang in there with me.

Answer this question: How full is your energy tank as you begin each day? Is it full, half-full, or close to empty? Imagine looking at your car's gas gauge as you answer this question.

_____

_____

_____

_____

_____

Wherever your energy gauge is each day, it can be fuller... the fuller the better for you, your child, your relationships, and all the other areas of your life.

Many of us believe consciously or subconsciously that mothers are supposed to be exhausted and last in line to eat and sleep. I, too, believed this crazy idea, which became a way of life for me.

The idea of self-compassion at first seemed selfish to me, but I discovered the bigger picture when it comes to loving yourself. I'm not saying don't care for others. I'm saying that in order to do that, you need to nurture your whole self while you care for others.

When you nurture and care for yourself as you do everyone else, you will change your life. You will not only build resilience, but you will also create balance and feel joy in your life again. You, like everyone else, deserve to feel loved and cared for in this life. We all do!

I hope you have not shut down the idea of putting yourself first and giving self-compassion a try. Take another breath, and stay with me just a little bit longer.

Kristin Neff, the Co-founder of the Center for Mindful Self-Compassion, explains that self-compassion is all about how we relate to ourselves and to others. Having compassion for oneself is really no different than having compassion for others. It is treating yourself as you would a close friend or a loved one.[2]

Self-compassion is not self-indulgent. No matter where you are on your journey, it's never too late to jump on the self-compassion train. I was in my fifties before I understood how important it is to practice self-compassion. It doesn't matter where you are or where you come from, just begin this life-changing practice now.

One of the first steps is to notice how you speak to yourself. I ask my clients to pay attention to their self-talk. We all talk to ourselves, whether we admit it or not. Take one whole day, and

---

[2] Neff, Kristin. Self-Compassion: *The Proven Power of Being Kind To Yourself.* Yellow Kite, 2011.

every time you talk to yourself, notice what you are saying. Is it positive or is it negative self-talk?

Write down some self-talk conversations that you have with yourself. What are you saying to yourself about yourself?

_____

_____

_____

_____

_____

_____

_____

_____

_____

_____

_____

_____

Now that you are aware of how you speak to yourself, begin to change the self-critic who lives inside of you to the beautiful loving nurturer that you can be.

Next, replace each negative self-talk response to a positive one. For example, I used to tell myself quite often, "Nice one Brigitte. That was so stupid. I am such a dummy." As I write these words, I feel sad about how I treated myself, without any awareness that I was speaking to myself so harshly. I would never speak to someone else like that, so why am I speaking so ugly to myself? With practice, I caught the negative self-talk, and I began to replace it with self-love talk.

Write down your negative self-talk and replace it with positive love self-talk.

_____

_____

_____

_____

_____

_____

_____

_____

_____

_____

_____

_____

_____

_____

_____

Neff explains what the experience of compassion feels like. First, you must notice that someone is suffering. If you ignore that homeless person on the street, you can't feel compassion for the difficulty of his or her experience.

Second, compassion involves feeling moved by others' suffering, so that your heart responds to their pain (the word compassion literally means to "suffer with"). When this occurs, you feel warmth, caring, and the desire to help the suffering person in some way. Having compassion also means that you offer understanding and kindness to others when they fail or make mistakes, rather than judging them harshly.

Finally, when you feel compassion (rather than pity) for another, it means that you realize that suffering, failure, and imperfection are all a part of the shared human experience.

Self-compassion involves acting the same nurturing way toward yourself as you do toward others. When you are having a difficult time, have failed, or notice something you don't like about yourself, don't just ignore your pain with a "stiff upper lip" mentality. Stop and take the time to tell yourself, "Things are really difficult right now; what can I do to comfort and take care of myself?"

Once on the Oprah Winfrey Show, I first heard the metaphor of flying on an airplane with my child when the plane loses control and the oxygen masks drop down. To whom do you give the oxygen mask first? Obviously, to my child, right? Wrong. I was shocked to learn that by the time I gave my child an oxygen mask, I would more than likely have lost consciousness and then who would help me? I would be no good to anyone unless I placed the oxygen mask on myself first. This is such a great example of how self-compassion practice is essential.

Now that you have begun practicing awareness, and replacing negative self-talk with positive self-talk, create a self-compassion mantra to give yourself the extra support you need to shift your inner critic to self-love and compassion. Self-compassion is all about accepting that you are not perfect and that is perfectly okay. Just as you accept others, you must accept your imperfect self.

I've asked you in each chapter to practice small acts of kindness as you work your way through this book. I believe that kindness is a superpower. If you agree that kindness is powerful, and that it can make a difference in another human being, then you can shift the direction of kindness to yourself.

We are all connected; together, we are part of the human experience. How we treat ourselves is essential to how we live our lives. Once you treat yourself with grace and love, your heart will expand and you will live with more joy and less fear.

Self-Compassion 101:

1. You know you are worthy of this practice if you are breathing. Take 3 deep breaths to remind yourself.

2. Make a list of all the self-love and kindness that you are craving. What are you daydreaming about? Write down any thought that pops up.

_____

_____

_____

_____

_____

_____

_____

_____

_____

_____

_____

Look at your list and don't judge it.
Every item on your list is possible.

3. Pick one item on your list. Now imagine that you are going to do this for someone else. Feel the positive energy.

4. In this good energy of giving to someone else, turn it around to yourself. Imagine giving yourself the self-compassion that you crave. Close your eyes and picture it.

5. Now just do it! Give yourself just one piece of self-compassion that you are craving. Next, write about the experience of turning compassion into self-love:

_____

_____

_____

_____

_____

_____

_____

_____

_____

_____

_____

_____

_____

_____

_____

You can continue this practice each day by picking one self-compassion act from your list of cravings. Gradually, you will become more and more skilled at self-compassion, and you will also begin to feel lighter.

If this sounds nice, and you are still resisting the act of self-love, make the self-love item smaller. For example, if you picked a hot meal, make it smaller by consuming a hot cup of coffee or tea. The most important piece of this exercise is that you take a breath and begin to nurture yourself. It doesn't have to be a big gesture, just the simple act of comforting yourself.

Take a few moments to define in your own words what self-compassion means to you. Then make a short list of how you would like to improve your self-compassion with a short list of intentional goals toward self-love:

_____

_____

_____

_____

_____

_____

_____

_____

_____

_____

Now, let's go a bit deeper with answering these questions:

Do you love yourself? List the evidence of your self-love. If the answer is no, then these practices are absolutely essential for you. Dig deep and find one small piece of anything that you love about yourself. Be gentle. Be kind.

_____

_____

_____

_____

_____

_____

_____

_____

_____

_____

_____

_____

_____

_____

_____

_____

_____

_____

_____

On a scale of 1-10, rate your level of self-compassion
(10 being the highest)

_____

How do you feel about your self-compassion rating?

_____

_____

_____

_____

_____

_____

_____

_____

_____

_____

_____

Where would you like the rating to be in a week, a month, six months, and then one year from now?

_____

_____

_____

_____

_____

_____

_____

As you move forward with growing your self-compassion practice, keep in mind that on some days, you may fall off the train, and that's okay. I fall off my self-compassion train frequently. I think it's important to remember that you are human, and you are learning how to love deeper each and every day. How you do that is up to you.

I recommend that you take one small step each day by remembering through your mantras a few small acts of kindness that put yourself first. This is how you will build your resilience and show up with fully charged superhero powers for your child.

Love is the essential reality and our purpose on earth. To be consciously aware of it, to experience love in ourselves and others, is the meaning of life. Meaning does not lie in things. Meaning lies in us.

- Marianne Williamson

12

Gratitude
and Reflection

As I have transformed from a person who almost always put others first and was extremely hard on myself, I found a daily practice that deepened not only my self-compassion but also my joy. Practicing gratitude opened up even more possibilities for me, and I think that it will for you too.

Gratitude, according to psychology research, is strongly and consistently associated with extended happiness. Showing gratitude can help people feel positive emotions, relish good experiences, improve their health, deal with adversity, and build strong relationships with more resilience and consistency.

Showing gratitude can drastically change your life, because that small act makes you appreciate what you have, rather than what you don't. It can also be the most powerful source of inspiration that any person can tap into if they simply just stop and pay attention to the beauty and miracle of life.

Daily gratitude practice:

Step 1: Before you get out of bed each morning, sit up and say 3 things that you are grateful for out loud. They don't need to be anything big. On some mornings, I am grateful for just the smell of my cup of coffee. On others, it may be for life itself. Once you have spoken and felt your gratitude, put your feet on the floor with the power of that gratitude for the upcoming day. I promise that you will notice a shift in how you begin each brand-new day full of possibilities.

Step 2: Once you can feel the gratitude, ask yourself who you want to show up as today. You can now choose to move to your favorite chair, lie in bed to do this step, or wait to put your feet on the floor after you have moved through all three steps.

On most of my days, I choose to be a person of service, although this can change. Being of service quickly brings me into who I want to be.

As you ask yourself this question each day, go with whatever comes up, and answer it from a place of gratitude that you have created. Use a declarative statement of who you want to be. For example, "I want to live this day as a person of service."

Step 3: Continue with your feelings of gratitude, while visualizing yourself doing one small act being who you have decided to be that day. Remember this is how you want to live your life for one day only. For example, I want to live this day as a person of service. I then close my eyes and I visualize myself in an act of service.

At first, begin with small acts and gradually expand them, as that feels safe and right. Maybe you are even thinking of a career change, but for today you are going to just edit your resume. If your act feels good, and you can stay in the feeling state of gratitude, then you know it's not too big. The act that you are visualizing needs to feel as comfortable as your favorite sweater.

Begin practicing these three steps each day. Use these tools all day long if you want to.

If you feel yourself losing the feeling of gratitude, take three deep breaths, and remind yourself who you want to be, and the feeling will most likely come back to you. Often, things that happen during the day challenge us. No problem...just notice the challenge, and take those three deep breaths.

I can say honestly that this practice has changed the way that I live each day. I no longer have to think about the steps or remind myself about beginning my day in gratitude. I just do the ritual each morning as simply as I brush my teeth.

These steps also allow me to live each day with purpose as the person I want to be by moving me forward one small step at a time. Once I am feeling positive, I know my purpose will take place, because I created it. I live in service and offer small acts of kindness, which in turn, generate feelings of love.

Many of my clients have told me how this activity changed their lives. What is so beautiful for me to hear is that they then share this practice with others, and together we are all spending our days in a much happier place.

I am filled with gratitude that I am a mother guide. I am grateful that I am traveling on a journey with my son, Joseph. I am grateful that I am having this life experience and that I am able to share it with other mothers.

In this place of gratitude, I ask you to ponder moving forward on this journey as a mother guide yourself. All of these chapters and practices that I have shared have been part of my own personal journey. When I began the first support group, my intention was to share resources, problem-solve obstacles, and support others. Writing this book continues that intention.

As I coach mother guides, I ask them to take a few moments and reflect on each session. The purpose is to help process the work together and to offer them support and comfort as each session ends.

Take a moment and find a safe space to write down these reflection questions.

What are some of the biggest take-aways that you can apply to your daily life from reading ***Mother's Guide Through Autism***?

_____

_____

_____

_____

_____

_____

_____

_____

_____

_____

_____

_____

_____

_____

_____

Moving forward, what daily practices will you follow from this guide? Remember to break practices down so they don't feel too big. Meet yourself where you are, and take small steps to move forward. Be kind and gentle with yourself.

My daily practices:

Monday: _____

_____

_____

Tuesday: _____

_____

_____

Wednesday: _____

_____

_____

Thursday: _____

_____

_____

Friday: _____

_____

_____

Saturday: _____

_____

_____

Sunday: _____

_____

_____

I have created a daily reflection from each of the chapters of **Mother's Guide Through Autism** to use. This daily reflection will allow you to quickly review as you move forward on your journey. This list is a quick reference for you on your difficult days. It can remind you that you and you alone can make a dark day a brighter day.

——

Mother's Guide Through Autism
Daily Reflection

Chapter 1 Daily Reflection:

Use your heart to guide you. You are a mother guide and you are specially made for your child. Feel the love that you have for your child. Love is the healing force that will comfort you when you are on your knees. Use the Mother Guide's Prayer or your own prayer (meditation), and know that the universe, angels, and God all hear a mother's prayer louder and clearer than any other prayer. Have faith and see the deep beauty in your child. Motherhood is unique and beautiful!

Chapter 2 Daily Reflection:

Your deepest fears are simply not true. Take comfort for now that this irrational belief or fear is not present today. Take a breath and recite this phrase or mantra. All is well at this moment.

Chapter 3 Daily Reflection:

There are no rules in healing your heart. Your pain is here to serve a purpose, to push you, and to teach you. What you resist will persist. Lean into it. Your pain is always present. Invite your pain in and take comfort in knowing that you can ask your pain to leave. Thank your pain and reflect on what pain has taught you each time you encounter it. Remember there is sunshine behind the dark clouds.

Chapter 4 Daily Reflection:

Hope is your north star. Today I look for signs of hope. Hope is always present. Once you have found where your hope is hiding, follow your hope out of darkness. Lean into Grief Mantra: Be Kind. Be Loving. Be Present. Comfort yourself today as you would your best friend. Use your hope to guide you through your grief into the light.

Chapter 5 Daily Reflection:

Use Your Daily Mantra to offer you support. Your daily mantra is essential to guide you whenever you start to doubt yourself, wonder whether you are capable of getting through your day, or just want to keep your life heading in a positive direction. Speak your mantra out loud, feel its words as you say them. Repeat it until you feel lighter. Feel the possibilities.

Chapter 6 Daily Reflection:

Today You Are Okay! Today you are okay to not be okay. Ask yourself if you are flowing with or against the current of life. Use a visual mantra to help accept what is, and flow with grace.

I am well, I am safe, I am grateful, I am.

Chapter 7 Daily Reflection:

Release Your Crazy Monkeys of Fear. Begin by imagining living today without fear. Breathe in, say the word "allow." When you exhale, say the word "surrender." With each breath, release your fear and live your life as if fear didn't exist. Put each crazy thought onto a cloud and watch as it drifts away. Your fearful thoughts are not real.

Chapter 8 Daily Reflection:

Let Kindness Be Your Superpower Today! Recharge your superhero powers with the simple prayer of asking for HELP: **H**ello **E**ternal **L**oving **P**resence.

Don't wait until your battery is drained to charge it. These daily practices are essential for your superpowers to stay charged.

Chapter 9 Daily Reflection:

There Is Always a Solution to Any Problem.
Move through each problem with kindness knowing that you will find the way. You are the advocate, the nurturer, the quarterback of your team. Have a game plan, and if the plan doesn't go the way you expected, then go back to the drawing board. Remember a plan is just a plan and can be changed. Hold onto hope and lead your team with kindness. Advocating with kindness is the proactive way to lead the path for your child.

Chapter 10 Daily Reflection:

"We must let go of the life we have planned, so as to accept the one that is waiting for us." – Joseph Campbell. Practice with one tiny step toward change. Accept the ones you cannot change today, and change the ones that you can. Today is what it is, beautiful.

Chapter 11 Daily Reflection:

Practice self-compassion. It is the overarching practice that makes your journey peaceful and joyful. Loving yourself each and every day guides your pathway and makes it lighter, brighter, and more purposeful. Begin with asking yourself what your spirit is craving. How will you feed your spirit? Put the oxygen mask on yourself first. Keep your self-love mantra filled with self-love talk. You yourself are enough when you remember to love yourself.

Chapter 12 Daily Reflection:

Find gratitude within yourself, and let the energy of gratitude enrich each day. Spend each moment of your day filled with deep appreciation for your life. The smallest pieces of gratitude will bring you joy.

Daily Practice for Each Chapter:

Give yourself small acts of kindness each and every day. Without loving kindness, you could lose your superhero powers quickly and suffer more greatly.

Use each of these daily reflections to remind yourself that you are on this mother guide journey. You are worth these practices to build your truth and resilience, heal your heart, and love more deeply. Continue to meet yourself where you are at as you move forward on your journey

I hope that this guide has offered you a safe haven to come to heal your heart, to recharge your superhero powers, and for your light to shine brighter.

Now that you have completed the mother's guide with me, flip the book over. We are using the design of this book as a metaphor for how different each of our perspectives can be living with autism.

I've shared my perspective as Joseph's mother guide, and Joseph, my son, will shine his light from his perspective of living life with autism. His hope is that he can offer you knowledge, support, and hope from the lessons he has learned along his own autism journey.

Autism is a journey, the goal is to enjoy the trip with love, patience and kindness.

- Brigitte

References

Kubler-Ross, Elisabeth. *On Death and Dying: What the Dying Have to Teach Doctors, Nurses, Clergy, & Their Own Families.* Routledge, 1969.

Neff, Kristin. *Self-Compassion: The Proven Power of Being Kind To Yourself.* Yellow Kite, 2011.

About
Brigitte M.
Volltrauer Shipman

Brigitte M. Volltrauer Shipman is an author, life coach, speaker, and teacher. She has thrived with her passion of coaching clients, and finding her best self through her life tsunamis. She specializes in coaching mothers who have children that are diagnosed with Autism Spectrum Disorder (ASD). This is Brigitte's second book; she is also the author of Is It A God Thing? She has thrived as an educator for more than twenty years. She holds a Masters Degree in Educational Leadership.

Being a mother is by far her greatest passion.

CPSIA information can be obtained
at www.ICGtesting.com
Printed in the USA
LVHW071628300422
717423LV00006B/18

Thank you for your support!

A Mother's Guide Through Autism Part II:
Through The Eyes of The Guided

Joseph D. Shipman

Writing Brave Press
547 North Avenue, Suite #173
New Rochelle, NY 10801
www.writingbravepress.com

Distributed by IngramSpark

Cover and Text Design: Karinna Klocko
Copyeditor: Meghan Muldowney & Patricia Lemer
Author Photos: Annika Friedland

Library of Congress Cataloging-in-Publication Data available.
ISBN 978-1-7375639-5-2 (paperback)
ISBN 978-1-7375639-6-9 (ebook)

First Edition

Acknowledgments

In the pursuit of writing this book, I'd like to give my thanks and acknowledgements to all of *my teachers and therapists,* especially *Mrs. Kathy Ducker* for writing the Foreword. They helped indulge my ability and desire to learn, so that I could become the person I am today. I'd also like to thank my current friends and loved ones, including my girl-friend and partner, *Kazia Davis*. They all, especially Kazia, are my support network and allies in independent living; I wouldn't be able to make it without them.

Most of all, in regard to the topics discussed, I'd like to thank *my mother and co-author.* This work would not exist without our collaboration, much less our close relationship. I thank her for all the encouragement, openness, and reminders that helped to complete this work. May the fruits of our labor bring benefit to all who encounter it.

*To my mom, the world's guides
(mother or otherwise), and everyone
on the spectrum*

———

Foreword
written by Mrs. Kathy Ducker

My career as a speech therapist offered me a variety of experiences doing therapy with both children and adults. My heart has always belonged to children, because I relate to them so well. Working with many different teachers provided additional opportunities that I will always treasure.

One teacher invited me to join a visit to her friend's house to observe her three-and-a-half-year-old son, Joseph. I saw a strikingly beautiful little boy, who was sitting at a desk and staring at a book. Since my love for children always overcame my sense of my surroundings, I immediately tried unsuccessfully to engage Joseph in conversation, but Joseph didn't look at me or respond to me in any other way.

Later that evening, I observed Joseph watching TV, and singing along with the bouncing ball on a children's show. He appeared to be reading the words, but I realized that he could have memorized them. Brigitte, Joseph's mother, informed me that Joseph had been reading words on the television and from books since he was 18 months old, even though he had difficulty making eye contact and using expressive language.

I think that Brigitte, a teacher herself, had suspected that Joseph was on the autism spectrum, but he had not been formally diagnosed. As a therapist, I recognized that Joseph did indeed display several characteristics of autism.

Since I worked in public schools, not in private practice, I was not at liberty to start any type of therapy with Joseph at that time. Joseph's parents sought out information from other agencies. They found that Joseph had above-average intelligence and some significant sensory issues. He was, as suspected, at the high end of the autism spectrum. When Joseph started kindergarten, he was evaluated by the school system and placed in speech/language therapy with me on a daily basis. He wasn't yet speaking in complete sentences, but he was an avid drawer.

He loved elephants, recognized the differences between Asian and African elephants, and drew them with details I had never noticed.

At each session, Joseph wanted to draw on the chalkboard, so I let him, and then we talked about his pictures. I modeled the sentences, and he repeated them. His artwork became more detailed every week. One day, he drew a three-ring circus, complete with horses, acrobats swinging on trapezes, and elephants performing tricks. "Amazing" doesn't even describe the talent of this young boy. Eventually, his language became more complex, and as it progressed, his art skills seemed to decrease.

Joseph was quite a fascinating little guy to work with, and eventually, he was talking quite well. As he moved through elementary and middle school, he needed therapy for understanding and using more complex and abstract language skills, such as idioms and voice inflections; reading facial expressions and emotions; initiating conversations with his peers; and responding appropriately in social situations. I continued working on his receptive and expressive language skills, as well as his sensory issues, and added new goals to target higher level skills.

I used "Social Stories" to help him understand how to respond appropriately in common social situations, such as asking for help. I became fascinated with Joseph and his rapid progress, and I soon became involved in a parent support group started by Joseph's parents. Most attendees were parents of children on the autistic spectrum. As I listened to their experiences, I learned more and more about autism. Learning about other children helped me help Joseph.

As the years went by, Joseph developed his skills, and his interactions with others improved. He occasionally had difficulties in classroom activities, like group projects, but overall was doing well. Academically, Joseph was above grade level in all areas. He read well and could enunciate words with perfect diction.

Fast forward several years. One afternoon, I walked into my local grocery store and saw a handsome young guy sacking groceries. It was Joseph! He always recognized me, so we began

a conversation. He, of course, spoke beautifully and was doing as well as any young person there!

I have also had the pleasure of hearing Joseph as an announcer on the local radio station. He was perfect for the job. His speaking abilities were excellent, as were his voice inflections. I felt so proud of him, knowing that he had found his niche.

Having the privilege to know and work with Joseph has been one of the highlights of my career. Now that I am retired, I reflect on those times working as a speech therapist in the public schools. I know that I learned more from the students than they did from me. Joseph Shipman will always hold a special place in my heart.

Kathy Ducker
Former Speech Therapist

Prologue

If you are reading this book right now, you're likely one or more of the following:

1. A mother or father guide with a child on the autism spectrum.

2. A friend or relative of someone who is either on the spectrum or caring for someone on the spectrum.

3. A curious person who wants to know about things related to autism and autistic people.

I believe there's a general question that applies to anyone reading this, which has to do with seeking information about autism from those who have a personal experience with it. Hopefully, you have already read, or will later read, the first half of this book, where my mom describes the ins and outs of raising me. She wisely imparts guidance for others in similar circumstances from a mother's point of view.

This part of the book comes directly from the perspective of someone on the spectrum. My purpose is to offer insight and knowledge into autism from someone who lives it. I am especially speaking to parental and guardian figures, or "guides," the term my mother and I like to call these special people.

My intention is to give a general guide as to how autism can manifest itself by recounting my life and experiences. I try to show how autism is an inherent part of my life and how important it has been to the formation of my identity. I don't intend this to be a comprehensive guide of "all things autism," but I do hope that my personal perspective can help anyone

reading this to figure out how to support their children, understand themselves, and/or understand autism generally.

I also give my opinions regarding certain topics related to general advice about helping people like me. In addition, I offer my point of view on how I believe autism should be addressed broadly, and how guides can or should participate in these causes. Unfortunately, this means that politics may be briefly brought up as a topic, so I apologize in advance for any discomfort this may cause.

Still, I think it's very important to cover all of these topics for this work to provide a level of information, perspective, and guidance that can be understood by anybody who reads it. I hope it will in some miniscule way help everyone who does. After all, I don't intend for this to be my first and final word on anything, much less on autism.

I will always do my best to learn and expand my understanding of any given subject I wish to talk about, especially something like autism, which has irrevocably colored my life and perspectives. If I discover that I'm wrong about anything in this book, I will correct it in some way later. I also will go out of my way to make sure that my perspective on any relevant topic is informed and set by right intentions, as it would be anything but beneficial or progressive if I was ignorant or motivated by ulterior motives.

With all of that said, I hope that you gain from this book anything that helps or guides you. I also thank you for even picking up this book in the first place. If you happen to either not like it or don't gain anything from it, I'd hope you'll find a way to pass it on to someone who might. Also keep in mind that I hope you read and experience much more than just this book. This is only one perspective, and as a wise person once said, "When you've met one person on the spectrum, you've only met one person on the spectrum." So, let's start with one person's beginning.

1

The First Steps

When I think back to my earliest memories, around three or four years old, they include having an ever-growing fascination with the people and things of the world. I also remember having subtle feelings that there was something inherently different about my experiences. Of course, my young understanding of these experiences and feelings wasn't exactly well-worded; it was visceral. Everything felt "normal." Yet, I knew that the way I processed the world around me was somehow different than it was for others, like my mom and dad.

That's why my mom and dad took me to a faraway town, got us a hotel room, and had me evaluated by these people who put incredibly loud headphones on my hypersensitive ears. I clearly remember the hotel, the beginning of my obsession with Dr. Seuss, and even specific parts of the day.

I later learned that hypersensitive hearing was one of the ways my autism manifested itself, and that the headphones were meant to reduce the pain I felt when I heard loud noises. The funny thing is that while wearing these headphones, I sometimes got to feed the ducks at a nearby pond. Oftentimes, I remember feeding the ducks more clearly than I remember the therapy itself. I suppose that's what my parents intended though, and that's part of what makes me feel incredibly fortunate that I was born to such thoughtful and dedicated people.

Indeed, this therapy didn't last forever, and after a week, we came back home. With us, we brought back a rather large cache of Dr. Seuss books and VHS tapes, which I read and re-read, and watched over and over. It seemed at times almost like I couldn't get enough of them.

Over the years I have acquired a large tape collection of dozens of movies, TV shows, and tapes with sing-a-long content.

Although I overcame most of my hearing sensitivity and started speaking more, the things I said were essentially sampled references to everything I had watched and read.

This scripted behavior is known by medical professionals as "echolalia," or as my parents started calling it, "video talk." I remember those years as a joyful but generally difficult period. While I don't recall a time in my life when I couldn't read written words, I do remember the feelings of frustration that came with trying to translate that knowledge into spoken, socially understandable communication.

For the life of me, I just couldn't seem to figure out why people had difficulty understanding what I was referencing. How could they not have known about Buzz Lightyear proclaiming he would go "to infinity and beyond"? How could it be that other people don't know the things I knew?

Luckily, these special needs would soon be addressed as I entered school. My mom just so happened to be a former first grade teacher, so every year until around fifth or sixth grade, she used her connections in our district to make sure I was assigned to a teacher she thought would be best for me. From there, my mother and the teachers worked together to make sure that I was integrated with other students socially and that I was also getting the special attention I needed to address my communication problems.

This support usually took the form of daily correspondence in journals between my mom, teachers, and speech therapist. These journals discussed my behavior and progress (or lack thereof). I clearly remember my speech therapy because it was a necessary diversion from my normal classroom activities. I got along so well with all the wonderful professionals who offered me the tools I needed to navigate social situations.

The activities we did together included puzzles, worksheets, games, and more direct social education, such as reading social stories. These are specially written scripts that show proper social behavior to children on the spectrum. In other words, in the same way some people hire a math or English tutor to

improve on those subjects, I had to be tutored on how to interact with other people. My mother made sure she was able to
oversee whoever was responsible for supplementing my development. I think she did a wonderful job with these therapists,
just as she had with my teachers. I can't remember a single
thing I ever disliked about anyone on my support team while
under their guidance.

I believe that my mom's supervision of my program is a
part of what helped each and every lesson and interaction
have a major impact. Some people might look at this method
of treating autism as some kind of behavioral conditioning,
sort of like a "dignified version" of dog training. However,
I would beg to differ. In my case, I felt totally supported,
because everyone was equally concerned about my navigation
of the world, not a strict conformity to the way others
navigated it.

Of course, some elements of coercion were sometimes
necessary, but I never considered any of their supervision to
be violent or abusive. They did not belittle my concerns or
interests. They always respected me fully and worked around
my personality, helping to empower me in a way that even
governs my life today. Insofar as my school career was concerned, this was just another class during my day.

As I assume it is for most children, the experiences of
my childhood felt universal. That is, although I knew that
certain aspects of my behavior and learning were different, I
did not feel that they were either developmental or medical
issues. My hearing sensitivities to the outrageously loud school
bell and fire alarm did not go away, and I still went to speech
therapy; these were just parts of my life. Eventually, over time,
I learned about why I was different. One day when I was
around eight or so, I went to speech therapy during school as
usual, and read a book about a young boy who was diagnosed
with something called "autism." The book went on to describe
how the boy couldn't talk very well and how he needed a lot of
help doing daily tasks. After reading it, I thought I had simply
read a story about a young boy who was living a fulfilling life,
despite having an unfortunate medical condition.

Later, when riding in the car with my mom, I decided I'd tell her about this book. My recollection of the book ended with me saying something like, "I sure felt sorry for him. I'm glad I'm not autistic like that." My mom simply replied, "But you are autistic." Naturally this blew my mind, but, as I said before, I had no such conception that the "autism" label applied to me. This revelation also humbled me. At the time, I didn't know about the ways in which autism can manifest in people. Compared to the boy I read about in that book, I was a relatively mild case. In some ways, I was not much like that young man, but he and I were also very much the same. Still, it couldn't be denied that from that point forward, the vague feeling of difference I felt became more familiar to me. As a result, I really started learning more about myself and about my condition. This is when I feel I truly started to grow as a human being and where my journey consciously began.

2

Signs & Symptoms

Negative sentiments towards self-referential labels, such as "autistic," are common, especially in relation to neurodivergent conditions. While I certainly agree that one should take care when qualifying oneself by strict categorization, labels exist because they can help bring certain things into perspective. Why your thoughts are patterned a certain way, why you seem to be frustrated with expressing yourself in a way few other people ever are, as well as being confused about the expressions of others – these can all be explained by knowing that you are on the spectrum. They all start to make more sense when all these experiences can be explained through a simple, shorthand term, such as "autistic."

A wariness toward labels is as old as language. This is especially true with labels that refer to phenomena that make humans generally uncomfortable, like those that refer to physical, genetic, or developmental differences. I remember frankly telling an adult faculty member about my diagnosis, shortly after learning that I was on the autism spectrum. I was more than happy to share my status with any open ear. My parents pulled me aside and explained that I should be careful of being so forthcoming, not out of shame, but because autism might be a difficult subject for people in this social situation.

I think this was the point when I began to achieve a greater social consciousness. I then began to pay more active attention to analyzing the social situation at hand (as I'd learned to do by reading the social stories) and modifying my behavior accordingly.

Today, I'm still quite open about my condition. When I tell people, they often respond, "I would have never known," or "You don't seem autistic." I can't help but take this as an innocent admission of ignorance as to what being "on the spectrum" really means.

While I will never deny the relative mildness of my autism, there's still an inherent difference in the brains of those on the spectrum that we all share: varying degrees of difficulty in communication and social interaction. Even though I'm pretty unhindered by my autism in daily life, much of my social behavior was crafted through direct therapy and intervention.

Children who are "neurotypical" usually pick up on the reasons for most social rules as if by instinct. Despite my affinity for social connection (a trait that some people on the spectrum lack), I had to learn the rules and customs directly, in the same way one is actively taught a particular skill or craft. Ironically, I can tend to be more socially conscious than some people. This can lead to other socially awkward moments, like having trouble communicating when I am caught off guard by the situation.

As I got older, I started noticing that I was often caught off guard. In the third grade, I got involved in an after-school program called Odyssey of the Mind (OM), that my parents coached. Odyssey of the Mind is an extracurricular program, founded in part by Dr. C. Samuel Micklus, which teaches K-12 students how to solve problems in a fun and creative way. OM's "seasons" involve assigning long-term problems that teams of students around the world try to solve. The teams then present their solutions in a competition.

I didn't exactly volunteer or ask to participate in OM, but since it looked like it would be fun, and I knew my parents would be there, I joined. That was a good decision, because not only did I enjoy it, but I found it was challenging and helped me learn more about myself and the unique way my mind worked. True to its name, the program helped me journey through the inner machinations of my mind and understand what made it different, yet still able to contribute to the project.

OM brought some of my struggles to light. One year, the problem to solve involved the use of idioms, which were extremely challenging for a kid like me, who took everything literally. Common expressions such as "it's raining cats and dogs" made me think that some people didn't understand reality.

I actually looked outside to see if there were cats and dogs falling out of the sky; I was confused as to why anyone would say something like that if it wasn't true in a literal sense.

Still, I was willing to learn, and I eventually did get the idea that sometimes people use idioms and hyperbole to express themselves. Even so, my performance at the competitions left something to be desired.

Once, I executed my presentation exactly the way I had practiced it to our makeshift audience of other kids in the program. What I hadn't understood, though, was that I would be facing actual judges, not my peers or a general audience. So, there I was, performing for the crowd, while my parents tried their best to get me to turn 45 degrees so I faced the same direction as everyone else. This brought up the additional challenge that I couldn't follow implicit directions. That is, if someone wanted me to do something, I needed (and sometimes still need) to be told directly.

Maybe I missed the explicit instruction to face the judges. I was really confused about what I was supposed to do. I felt kind of stupid for not getting it and having everyone be frustrated with me not understanding the implicit social cues they had instinctually understood. I felt bad that it hurt us competitively. Despite my difficulties, I'm still glad I was in Odyssey of the Mind. I feel that my time there really helped me begin to understand the subtleties of expression in language.

I can recall many other instances where I learned something more about who I am and how my mind works. I think one of the main reasons I was able to develop a strong sense of social self-awareness was due to the very healthy support system I had as a child.

It's really hard to make sense out of the way you think and act if you don't have people who want to help you be the best version of yourself, who will help you reflect on your perceptions. I was so fortunate to have a team of people who advocated for me when I couldn't. These individuals worked with me instead of against my autism.

It is the absolute truth that it takes a village to raise a child, and it's even more important when a child has deficits in social skills/development. Despite the peaks and valleys that typically exist within every family, village, town, city, or country, my support network of relatives, professionals, and other just plain nice people was as strong as it could have been for my small mountain town. Today, as I look back, I feel quite fortunate indeed. I want to give back, so I make it a part of my life's mission to share my good fortune.

Too many people like me reach adulthood without knowing how to express themselves well. Often, whatever expressions they can muster are hindered by a lack of support. This is sometimes the result of poor access to help for special needs or a lack of effort to build or sustain a community in the first place.

I believe we can greatly change society so that it allows access for more people on the spectrum to have the materials and relationships they need. Without support, it is difficult, and sometimes impossible, for parents, teachers, medical professionals, peers, or people on the spectrum to recognize the signs or symptoms.

3

On The Downside

Autism, and other developmental disabilities, can be a difficult topic for many people to tackle. This is especially true for those who have an experiential understanding of the challenging side of life on the spectrum. As much as it makes people uncomfortable to bring up the negative side of autism, it's almost like the elephant in the middle of the room, because it's on many people's minds. Let's go ahead and address the downsides.

I want to be clear; I consider my experience with being on the spectrum as especially fortunate, considering the relatively mild nature of my autism, the time and place in which I was diagnosed, and my socio-economic circumstances. Given my good fortune, I would attribute most of the downsides of my experience to be the negative aspects of a close-to-best-case scenario.

I cannot, nor will not, attempt to equalize the experiences of all people with autism. Though I will touch on the struggles we all share, and should be aware of, my observations are mostly about some of the challenges I experienced. Hopefully, what I am writing will be informative and helpful to anyone going through similar circumstances.

First, I'll discuss the aspects of my autism which no longer affect me in the way they once did and why I think I'm now less affected. I touched on some of these in the first chapter, but now I'll go into deeper detail.

While the therapy I received back in that faraway town was incredibly helpful in my development, and reduced the sensitivity of my hearing, it didn't totally eliminate it. I remember certain instances where my highly sensitive auditory processing impacted me when going to places like movie theaters.

In one such instance, a trailer for the then-upcoming Star Wars film, The Phantom Menace, was so loud that I screamed out loud for the theater to turn down the sound. Unfortunately, when they turned down the volume as much as they could, others couldn't hear it. Despite this incredibly kind cooperation, the sound was still unbearable for me and I noticed no perceptible difference.

My mom and I solved the problem by standing outside until the feature presentation came on. What sticks with me most is that I am still fearful of any potential spike in volume. My fear is not just of the loudness, but also of my reaction to it being judged by others.

Even if I couldn't navigate or understand a lot of social mores back then, I remember having been taught how to control the volume of my voice in social settings, so as not to disturb others. I also remember frequently having a gut feeling whenever events like this came up, because it flustered my mom.

When I think back on it, I don't believe that she was embarrassed by me, but rather she was still learning about my quirky behavior and development. She didn't want others to see me as something I wasn't, to intervene in a way that would exacerbate my problems, or hinder my development.

This wasn't the only event when fear of high volume set me off. For example, what should have been an entirely fun experience at the opening of an IMAX theater was dampened by my fear of the sound being too much for me. By this point, I knew to cover my ears whenever I anticipated loud noises. Still, I had a wonderful time, and I was taken in by the immense size of the screen and the grandiose nature of the images being shown.

Even though I now recognize that my experiences with sensory overload aren't as severe as they are for some others on the spectrum, I would have loved it if I didn't have to actively worry about my overly reactive senses back then. Hopefully once the COVID-19 pandemic becomes less severe, I'll be able to indulge in the powerful presentation of an IMAX movie once again.

These specific incidents are somewhat different from the loud noises I have had to deal with on a daily basis. I have always hated the surprise blaring of the fire alarm for fire drills or the bells that rang for the end or beginning of certain periods. Thank goodness my reaction to both, especially the fire alarm, has gotten less severe over time, yet for someone like myself, it sometimes still feels like overkill.

If I possessed the verbiage back then, I would have likened it to a sonic weapon, specifically designed to make ears bleed. My tentative relationship with loud sounds continued to some degree up until around sixth or seventh grade. By that point, I had acclimated to most daily sounds and their occasional spikes or dips in volume.

Today, I am happy to report I am pretty typical in the way I process sounds. This is fortunate, because, as I am writing this chapter, my significant other and I are taking in her brothers and sisters, while their parents are in quarantine for the afore-mentioned pandemic.

I want to explain my ability to communicate and navigate social interactions, as this is one of the most significant and well-known aspects of autism. This aspect is one that is much less severe in its effect on me now than in the past. First, another victory is that I haven't engaged in echolalic speech since late elementary school. Sometimes it's hard to recall the timing of some of the memories related to this period, because the way I communicate now is so alien to my poor communication skills back then.

What I remember though are multiple instances when I became rather obsessive about a piece of media I had heard and quoted it constantly. This "talking" provided the content for my interactions with others for quite some time, even when my parents frequently reminded me that not everyone knew some of the things I was talking about.

I can still hear them saying things like, "Remember what we said about video talk?" and "party for one" (referring to the fact that I was referencing something only I knew in a social

context, but no one else was in on the reference). As odd as it might sound to many people, I would often forget that people didn't operate on the same set of information as I did. I didn't always have "theory of mind," and I required considerable support and coaching to be able to understand that concept. I eventually came to learn how to monitor myself, but as I said before, it felt more like something I had learned from a book or a class, rather than something picked up instinctually. Fortunately, I have a pretty good memory and a love of learning, and I think I always will.

Even though a few other earlier aspects of my autism no longer negatively affect me much, I will stop there for now. After all, if I recalled every instance in detail, this half of the book would be longer than all of Shakespeare's works combined. So, I will move on to describing some of the struggles I still face from time to time.

Like many on the spectrum, I also have sensory issues with texture, particularly with food. This is one of the reasons I avoid eating all spuds (for example: potatoes, sweet potatoes, yams, fries, and chips). Another reason for avoiding these foods is that they have never agreed with me. Every time I tried to eat a potato, I felt nauseous or had a similarly negative reaction.

My avoidance of spuds might have even caused me to develop an allergy to them. When I tried peeling potatoes a few years ago, I developed a scratchy throat and difficulty breathing. Luckily, I stopped peeling before I found out how bad the reaction could have been.

Although as an adult I don't struggle much with social interaction, I sometimes have trouble with understanding. I consider these present struggles to be mostly on par with those of neurotypical people, but if there's one thing that's still different, it's the fact that I tend to get nervous during conversations. Although I wouldn't change the path I took to my present self, I think that one unintended side effect of my struggles was making me socially hyper-aware. If I feel that I've made a faux-pas or miscommunicated especially poorly, I still tend to experience some anxiety, especially if I hurt someone unintentionally.

As a result of wanting to avoid this outcome, I tend to be somewhat insecure in certain relationships. Instead of over-explaining some movie or TV show no one except me had seen, I now tend to over-explain what I say to avoid any harmful or inaccurate interpretation. I do this to avoid being an annoyance, but ironically, this can still make me annoying sometimes.

Even as I compose this book, I am having some self-judging thoughts running in the back of my head, like antivirus software in my brain. This speaks to the fact that some people on the spectrum pay more attention to social cues/mores than neurotypical people. I feel this is because we have to consciously observe our interactions through a much more cerebral, less instinctual approach to making sure we're on good terms with people.

I feel that this hypervigilance tends to be truer for the extroverted people on the spectrum like me. That might sound strange to some readers, as being both extroverted and autistic is not the typical stereotype.

Unfortunately, I have developed what I think may be symptoms of social anxiety. I'm not anxious about social interaction in general, but rather I tend to worry about any interaction potentially being misconstrued as negative or not exactly as I intended. Lately I've feared accidentally saying or expressing thoughts that could alienate people.

If there's anything else I would really consider to be a downside to having autism, it would be how society in general, and some people in particular, view and treat those on the spectrum. Indeed, there are many challenging inherent aspects of autism, but many of us also have to deal with both our own idiosyncrasies and the way neurotypical society reacts to us and our autism.

This type of hurdle comes from a variety of different places. It comes from people who are ignorant about or who have negative perceptions of autism; it also comes even from those who ostensibly want to help us. As I've said, I feel that the particular characteristics of my autism are relatively mild, in part

because my parents worked incredibly long and hard to find services for me. Even though the small town I grew up in didn't have many options for services, my parents traveled to far reaches of the country to find specialists who could help me. My mom has, on several occasions, told me how she had to contact people as far away as Boston to find a specific service. They even had to go out of state to get me a proper diagnosis. I don't even think I would have gotten the help I needed at school if my mom hadn't been a teacher who knew all the teachers in my district. She was able to hand-pick who would be the best for me.

I only realized how fortunate I was after the fact, and I imagine that some who are reading this book could not afford or access the services that they or their children needed. While we may not be able to totally mitigate all symptoms for every person on the spectrum, I believe we can change things for the better by making care, attention, and resources more readily accessible.

I understand this may be a difficult chapter to read. However, if we acknowledge the material, social, and inherent negative realities of autism, the better we'll be able to address these problems, and, just as importantly, celebrate those things about autism which make us special and enrich all of our lives.

4

On The Upside

Let's talk about some of the upsides of being on the spectrum. Even though it has its downsides, it's most certainly not all bad. This might sound like a strange way of looking at autism, but I believe that some of my traits are a boon to experiencing life.

My father told me that my grandmother had once asked him if he thought that someday there would be a cure for autism. He said he told her that even if he had a magic wand that could change me, he wouldn't use it. He didn't think of autism as something that was wrong with me, just that I was a little different, and that was okay with him.

Many people with autism, including me, develop very intense interests in particular subjects. In my case, it's been many things, from elephants and horses, to…well, game shows. Even to this day I can get lost in a subject, thinking that only an hour has passed, when it was actually four.

When I was in third grade, and the teacher assigned us to give a presentation about how seeds make plants grow, this trait served me very well. Initially, I had a difficult time coming up with a way to present my assignment. My father suggested using my obsession with TV game shows to present make the assignment as into a game show. We glued seeds to answer cards and made corresponding question cards; we then created a poster board with name and score spaces.

Not only did I get an A+++ grade (yes, my teacher actually gave me an A with three pluses) on the assignment, but my classmates and I had a really good time engaging in the presentation that my dad and I had created. I think I was able to accomplish this not just because of my parents' support; I was also able to use my focus, innate creativity, and interest in delving deeply into a specific subject.

I view my ability to focus intently as a gift. I love learning new things, and some people seem to think I know a great deal. Even though that might be true, I know there's always more to learn, and that's exciting to me. Fortunately, being able to learn relatively easily and quickly has also helped me do well in my daily life, such as when taking on a new job, learning how to pay a bill, and even meeting and interacting with new people. All of these things would be immensely more difficult if I wasn't able to acquire and retain information the way I do. I find this is a trait many people on the spectrum have in common as well.

This inquisitive tendency has also allowed me to use my imagination in understanding the world around me. Because I had to learn about human interaction through a more informational style, I have developed a "third party" view of society and culture in general. That is, I observe like a scientist while still being a part of the phenomena I'm observing. This has led to my ability to be open-minded and passionate about helping people, while also being socially and politically critical.

Environmental activist Greta Thunberg and I share these autistic gifts. Originally from Sweden, Greta began to develop a deep motivation for spreading awareness about climate change at around age 8. By the time she was 15 or 16, she was leading student strikes and directly criticizing those in power who were doing little to mitigate or confront climate change.

Throughout this time period, she experienced deep depression and was also diagnosed with Asperger's syndrome. Like me, she has acknowledged some of the limitations of being on the spectrum, and, at the same time, she calls her autism a "superpower." I honestly couldn't agree with her more.

I can't think of too many neurotypical people who could or would challenge political leaders' inaction towards climate change to their face. Frankly, given the existential weight of the issue of climate change, Thunberg's outspoken and direct manner on this subject is sorely needed. While most people would be hindered by social mores and an avoidance of speaking directly about uncomfortable topics, Ms. Thunberg clearly is not.

I consider it a blessing that not only is this young woman one of the most well-known climate activists, she is one of the most widely known autism activists in the world. As far as I'm concerned, she represents our best interests. By "our," I don't just mean people on the spectrum, but humanity at large. If we are truly fortunate, Greta will one day be known as one of the greatest humanitarian figures of the 21st century.

Despite common negative stereotypes, most people on the spectrum not only care about others, but also have a deep intolerance for injustice. I think that humans all have a certain innate sense of justice, but this trait can be rather profound with people on the spectrum. As social creatures, humans derive information from each other through social means. I wonder if this is a reason why so many neurotypical people mistake our lack of understanding of social cues, or difficulty in engaging, as evidence of a lack of empathy or just being antisocial.[1]

As I mentioned, I'm a more extroverted autistic person, and I understand those who might be more introverted. I believe that when people on the spectrum avoid interaction, it is out of fear of how they might be received rather than how they personally feel about associating with others. Even though some are more introverted, all seem to me to be steadfast in their humanitarian, intellectual, and ethical values. Many are passionate about causes they feel are beneficial to humanity.

If anyone on the spectrum sees someone being treated unfairly, their reactions, including mine, are deep and strong. Reactions can range from a social meltdown to vehemently speaking out against a specific injustice. Though this behavior can sometimes lead to incorrect conclusions, few to no responses are motivated by a lack of care or desire to be friendly and respectful to others.

I have frequently beaten myself up for unintentionally saying something wrong or hurtful. I'm told sometimes I am a bit hard on myself. I also often try to be of benefit or to promote what seems good. I've stood with others like me, baffled by the hypocrisy of militantly "moral" people preaching against doing a thing that would promote the very values they claim to support.

[1] Kapp, Steven Kenneth. *"Social Justice and Autism: Links to Personality and Advocacy."* Dissertation. University of California, Los Angeles, 2016. https://escholarship.org/uc/item/

These values have led me to pledge my support to various worthy causes. I have joined and worked for a variety of organizations throughout my life and am especially active today.

I think I share strong levels of conviction with Greta Thunberg and others on the spectrum. It certainly takes a remarkable level of conviction to do what Greta does, and to ask world leaders to their faces how they dare do nothing about our desperate climate emergency. We may not be able to tell what others are feeling or thinking sometimes, but we do still care about other people and we will always do what we think is right, period.

People on the spectrum share some traits, but not all. Despite the unique difficulties that come with our developmental disability, I try hard to understand reactions from those with disorders or anyone who cares for them. Different perspectives are needed in order to see the whole. That's why I'm glad there has never been a magic wand or any other method to undo and reverse engineer my autism.

I have always been able to have my needs addressed in a way that has allowed me to be my quirky, mysterious self. Everyone, autistic or not, no matter how mild or severe their disability, deserves to have their needs met, so they can become their most authentic true selves. We are all valuable and special human beings, who can live happy, meaningful, and fulfilling lives.

5

Going Forward

One valuable lesson I have learned and taken to heart in my almost 30 years of living with autism is that once we discover our individual and joint needs, and what effects they have on our lives, we should take action. I now want to express my personal views on how autism should be addressed, in the hopes that it will help others forge their own paths. I want to stress that these are my personal opinions and views, and they are based on factual information. I cannot and do not speak for the experiences of others.

The most important part of addressing autism, in my opinion, is to have a strong support network, composed of family, friends, medical professionals, acquaintances, and virtually everyone that can have a positive influence. I don't mean that you need to get a huge number of people. Rather, I just mean that you need to assemble a dedicated bedrock of folks connected through mutual interests and feelings of love. Clearly, it takes a village to raise any child, special needs or not.

I have absolutely no idea how my autism could have been addressed if I hadn't had so many loving and supportive people around me to guide me through life. Inarguably, parents, grandparents, siblings, aunts, and uncles are invaluable building blocks. They are the first to provide aid, nourishment, and guidance.

Extended and immediate family must learn about autism in general, how it manifests in their loved one, and what positive steps they can take to address it. They also need to know how to access necessary resources, local or not, and be able to advocate for their loved one, as well as for those who are similarly affected. After all, it is in all of our best interest to aid those in need to the extent that we can. While a few of the traits that autism

manifests are difficult to mitigate, working with them tirelessly over time can increase both quality and length of life. My family and many families I've come to know are incredibly dedicated and good people who try their hardest to do what they think is best for their loved ones. As I touched on, the town I came from didn't have many available resources back when I was diagnosed, so my mom and dad had to search the whole country to find help for me.

My parents attended out-of-state conferences and consulted with distant practitioners. This required that we stay in hotels for cutting-edge therapies when I was young. They purchased an expensive desktop computer with an internet connection and educational games for me. They did just about everything they could think of to help me.

One thing I am very grateful for is that my caretakers and especially my parents didn't try to change or suppress my special interests like watching game shows. They viewed these obsessions as non-harmful, just plain "different" traits. I think that this approach helped connect me to other adults who contributed to the development of my present self. I sincerely don't think that I would be who I am today without that support. I always felt totally accepted and cared for.

Of course, everyone's resources and paths toward adulthood are different. I believe that any method that addresses a healthy way to help a person on the spectrum should be implemented. I support funding social programs that promote awareness of any signs of abuse in the home or school. It's paramount that everyone be connected to a fundamental social network. For anyone who has difficulties in sensory perception, and especially social development, a good family is damn near everything.

Educators, therapists, and anyone else who imparts knowledge of any kind are also extremely important as team members for someone on the spectrum. All must be knowledgeable about various developmental and learning disabilities, as well as the behaviors they manifest. Quite honestly, I can't imagine that my situation could have been any better. All of my grade school

teachers up until fifth grade were hand-picked by my mom, who had been a first-grade teacher. Everyone knew my speech therapist, who wrote the Foreword to this book. Any and every accommodation that anyone could think of was "on the table," if it could possibly make my life easier.

One great idea was to use a notebook in which my teachers wrote updates about my day. I think that my mom still has a few of these notebooks. I have read through them, remembering fondly (and not-so-fondly at times) how I used to be. It's absolutely amazing to recall all the wonderful lessons I've managed to use even now and how much I've grown as a person.

It is therefore that I think teachers and parents must collaborate to assure that every student with special needs receives an education that respects and bolsters their personhood. I strongly believe that families must be consistently informed about how their child is doing at school.

Just as people with autism need to have a supportive social network within the community, they need to have one within the school system as well. Their education should extend to making sure that they get what they need in order to continue learning and growing throughout their lives. Families must have access to good educational programs and resources. People on the spectrum need to be included, seen, listened to, and empowered in the planning of their education. If school districts need resources, they should have them. We should fund and encourage students to join extracurricular activities or after-school programs. All teachers, educational professionals, and therapists should also have budgets for materials and resources, as well as much higher pay and benefits. We should make strong efforts to mitigate possible reasons a person on the spectrum might not be receiving their due education. That could include addressing comorbid conditions, socio-economic circumstances, or other impediments to their learning.

I think it will become increasingly important for communities to address large-scale social, economic, and political issues that affect special needs populations; they should also advocate for those on the spectrum in these arenas.

These issues are all interconnected. Most people belong to multiple identities or groups, and the groups have many common needs. No man is an island and humans aren't solitary creatures. I am generally supportive of organizations and causes that advocate for autism awareness and acceptance. There has been a drastic increase in the rate of diagnosis of autism over the past three decades. When I was diagnosed in 1995, the rate was 1 diagnosis for every 150 children. The latest figures from the CDC show a rate of 1 in 44.

This begs the question: Why are rates of diagnosis for Autism Spectrum Disorder (ASD) skyrocketing? The totality of reasons for this is complicated and some aspects are debated. According to a 2017 article published in Scientific American, a large portion of increased diagnosis is attributable to:

1. Changes in diagnostic criteria
2. Increased overall awareness of autism.

In my lifetime, the criteria for diagnosis have changed twice, and it may change again as we learn more. Dr. Maureen Durkin, Professor and Chair of Population Health Sciences at the University of Wisconsin-Madison, said, "Until the 1980s, many people with autism were institutionalized, rendering them effectively invisible. Studies show that parents who are aware of autism's presentation—by living near someone with the condition, for example—are more likely to seek a diagnosis for their children than parents with no knowledge of the condition. Living close to urban centers and having access to good medical care also boost the likelihood of diagnosis." The article also notes that some causes can be biologically determined. Having an older father or being born prematurely are thought to increase the likelihood of an ASD diagnosis.[2] That's why I believe it is so important that people continue advocating for more awareness about autism. As the public has become increasingly conscious of autism, medical and psychological knowledge have expanded, leading to a better understanding of the needs of individuals with this disability. This knowledge has led to more acceptance and a decrease in stigma, resulting in an overall increase in benefit for individuals on the spectrum and those caring for them.

Although general awareness about autism has certainly increased, I think more is still needed in the future. Increasing awareness is also incredibly valuable for groups who have had historically less access to knowledge and resources, due to systemic inequalities and discrimination. For example, according to the CDC 2021 Community Report on Autism, there are still current efforts to continue closing the gap between racial groups, as rates for diagnosis are still disproportionately lower for Black and Hispanic children than for white children. This is often due to lack of awareness, racial stereotypes, and disproportionate access to resources.[3]

Of course, not all who advocate on our behalf have the same perspective on how to approach making the world a better place for people on the spectrum. As with any group, a diversity of thought and action exists among those in the autism community.

One of the biggest debates in the past decade has to do with the rise of the neurodiversity movement and the discourse it has inspired. Proponents of the neurodiversity movement, as related to ASD, argue that autism and its various traits should not be pathologized, but rather seen as an inseparable part of one's identity that should be accepted, rather than cured or eliminated.

They argue that autism is a manifestation of the myriad types of brain structure, and all efforts should be made to bring forth acceptance of autism as a difference, in the same way we recognize the importance of biodiversity among species and environment. Given this, they argue autism's over-medicalization leads many traits to be disabling; autism-friendly environments and cultural norms of acceptance can minimize disabilities and even allow some traits to manifest as useful skills or talents. Therefore, many in the movement believe that the way autism is seen and treated by the medical world and society is harmful to people on the spectrum. They criticize some methods of treatment as dehumanizing or even as an existential threat to autistic people as a group, akin to eugenics.[4]

3 Center for Disease Control. *"Spotlight On Closing the Racial and Ethnic Gaps in the Identification of Autism Spectrum Disorder among 8-year-old Children."* CDC, 2 December 2021. https://www.cdc.gov/ncbddd/autism/addm-community-report/spotlight-on-closing-racial-gaps.html

4 Baron-Cohen, Simon. *"The Concept of Neurodiversity Is Dividing the Autism Community."* Scientific American, 30 April 2019. https://blogs.scientificamerican.com/observations/the-concept-of-neurodiversity-is-dividing-the-autism-community/

Critics of the movement often argue that support for the neurodiversity movement often comes from and puts the spotlight on a narrow group of people on the spectrum who have mild to benign symptoms. They point out that despite the claim to speak for people on the spectrum as a whole, this focus ironically excludes many people whose symptoms are severe enough to warrant treatment and analysis through a medical lens. Also, they point out that this exclusion of voices leads to unintentionally taking focus and resources away from those with a much higher demand for care. This ignores how often many on the more severe side of the spectrum may lament their condition.

I consider myself to be a proponent of neurodiversity as a concept, as I think it brings attention to the fact that people with disorders or disabilities are often marginalized by society and either untreated or mistreated as a result. In the history of autism, there have been numerous instances of reaching conclusions or supporting treatments that not only don't help anyone, but may even exacerbate certain traits negatively and lead to wider prejudice and dehumanization.

One example comes from some of the work of Dr. Leo Kanner, not only the first person to identify "autism" as we understand it, but the first child psychiatrist in the United States. In particular, he published his major work Autistic Disturbances of Affective Contact in 1943. This was a scientific case study paper which argued that children withdrew into themselves because parental figures were cold to their children. This led to the idea that children were, in a sense, "made" autistic by their parents not showing enough affection.[5] This came to be called "refrigerator mother theory" and was the predominant narrative about autism until around the 1970s. Despite clarifications and changes to this notion by Kanner himself, this led to many parents being told to institutionalize their children, a practice that was unfortunately common for just about any physical, mental, or developmental disability.

Of course, this change in the 1970s wasn't equally true for everyone. I was recommended for institutionalization when I was suspected to be on the spectrum…and this was in the mid-1990s. Even now, many people with any sort of divergent

5 Cohmer, Sean. *"'Autistic Disturbances of Affective Contact' (1943), by Leo Kanner."* Embryo Project Encyclopedia, Arizona State University, 23 May 2014. http://embryo.asu.edu/handle/10776/7895

neurology are subject to ignorant stereotypes at most benign to outright discrimination or neglect at worst. I'm grateful that my parents took an approach that treated what needed to be treated, while still respecting my differences and interests, and therefore my humanity.

I'm not sure how well-adjusted I would be if I were treated the same way the disabled or differently-abled have been treated historically. I fear I would have suffered a grim, lonely fate had it not been for the balanced approach of my parents and my particular network of loved ones, friends, and professionals.

The neurodiversity movement deserves credit for focusing on promoting the voices and rights of people who have historically lacked a voice. They also deserve credit for calling out methods of treatment which they believe only address changing superficial behaviors. They advocate against methods that are dehumanizing or unethical, or methods that deny the autistic person any other desires or needs they might have.

I will always stand up for anyone being personally or systematically marginalized, and I will always promote our inclusion in ideas or movements about us. I fundamentally agree with the slogan, "Nothing about us, without us."

I should point out, though, that I support those who are still struggling for understanding and acceptance. I believe it's reductive to promote the idea that all of us are latent geniuses who don't have any real disabilities, but are rather just quirky. Furthermore, stereotypes about those on the spectrum being generally less capable in some areas are also wrong.

These are overcorrections which are understandable, but they can promote a sort of denialism in regard to the struggles some people on the spectrum face. Ironically, it's an inverse, positive-sounding dehumanization. It creates new stereotypes that still exclude the voices and needs of those of us who bear great struggle, who for very understandable reasons do not see their being on the spectrum as any sort of "superpower" or "gift." I fully promote the idea of diversity in human neurology and an end to all oppression and marginalization, but we must

also make sure to look out for these aforementioned errors. We should continue to challenge harmful, dehumanizing narratives about us. We should promote our involvement and input in research, advocacy, and organizing. We can also ensure we don't invalidate any person's experiences or needs, and we should build bridges with the medical community and others to find solutions that lead all of us down a good road.

Here is a list of some organizations that I think do good work in both recognizing observed medical realities and promoting the autonomy, well-being, and voices of people on the spectrum:

- Autistic Self-Advocacy Network (USA)
- National Autistic Society (USA)
- Thinking Person's Guide to Autism (USA)
- Autistic Inclusive Meets (UK)
- Communication First (USA, International)
- The Autistic Cooperative (International)
- Yellow Ladybugs (AU)
- Autistic Women and Nonbinary Network (USA, focus on LGBT+)

These organizations all have direct input or involvement from people on the spectrum, including employing autistic people in leadership positions. They, and organizations with similar approaches, are ones I consider worthy of support. Of course, be wary of any organization that promotes outdated or scientifically unfounded claims or excludes input from those on the spectrum or their loved ones. We are all in the same boat, even if we may be in different sections.

As such, I think it will become ever more important to look at wider policy issues that affect everyone and those of us on the spectrum disproportionately. One such issue that needs attention is public access to healthcare, including universal healthcare. The financial burdens of people on the spectrum and their loved ones are huge. These can be compounded if someone on the spectrum has any other disorder or illness

(which is incredibly common among those with ASD), or is generally neglected by society.[6] They may not even have enough to purchase a book like this one. I totally support policies that divert funds into providing for those with special needs in public educational institutions and investing in community infrastructure (especially in low-income areas).

Another idea I have is to make advanced communication technologies for those who are nonverbal readily available on computers, tablets, and smartphones. The latest technology can help many nonverbal people overcome their limitations in communicating with the world.

Too often, people with severe symptoms are pitied and sympathized with, only to be ignored by larger efforts or discourse within and without the autism community. We often get caught up in the struggles they face, and we forget that they are human beings underneath the symptoms. It's important to recognize and accept those things that we cannot change. We can also work within certain limits, so that we can unlock the person without inflicting harm on them.

Carly Fleischmann is a great example of the success of this approach. She is a young woman who was diagnosed with autism, as well as general developmental delays and oral-motor apraxia, which rendered her nonverbal. After many years of treatment, her parents discovered that she could communicate by typing into a computer and later by using a tablet with special software. Carly's story received great media attention. She gained fame, not just for shattering many stereotypes about autism, but also for her extremely outgoing personality and insightful perspectives. She has recently gained a large social media following, including a YouTube channel talk show, on which she hosts interviews with celebrities like Channing Tatum and Stephen Colbert.

Unfortunately, Carly's channel has been inactive for some time now, amid allegations of her being silenced by her family and their staff. Whatever may actually be the reason, I hope that Carly is healthy, happy, and able to freely express herself again soon.

---

6 Rogge, Nicky, and Juliette Janssen. *"The Economic Costs of Autism Spectrum Disorder: A Literature Review."* Journal of Autism & Developmental Disorders, vol. 49, no. 7, 2019, pp. 2873-2900. https://link.springer.com/article/10.1007%2Fs10803-019-04014-z

Carly's important story is only one of many that shows the potential to look beyond "disability" and find "ability." We don't need to "fix" people on the spectrum. Instead, let us help them overcome their limitations and address their special needs, while respecting their differences, interests, and personality. Carly, and many like her, may not be able to speak as I can, but we all have voices worth sharing, as long as we all work towards those ends. We can and should treat what needs to be treated, without the unfortunate tendency of marginalization and dehumanization by society that has often come with having special needs.

I feel we should focus our energies on lifting up everyone we can. Obviously, we can't expect autistic people or their guides to do everything and anything outside of their self-care. However, we can recognize that any work in the right direction is good work. Doing what we can to improve larger societal and political responses to those on the spectrum and otherwise is self-care.

Even if someone ends up needing to support positions or organizations they may not have considered or even agree with, it might be necessary for their personal and collective benefit. After all, society is about all of us! Society is all of us! Observe what works and what needs to be changed. Improving someone's life improves everyone's lives. It will be worth it in the end, as it always has been.

7 Chomhaill, Nadia Nic Giolla. *"Family Of Missing Social Media Star, Carly Fleischmann, Says She Is 'Doing Well.'"* Unwritten, 14 January 2021. https://www.readunwritten.com/2021/01/14/family-missing-carly-fleischmann/

6
Conclusions

I hope that this half of the book has been helpful and informative. If it has, I'm happy, and I thank you for reading. I hope that I've laid out a broad and accurate recollection of my past and present life experiences on the autism spectrum.

My intent, first and foremost, is to give mother guides a hopeful outlook on the quality of life of their children. Next, I aim to help mother guides forge their own paths. Finally, my goal is to empower those on the spectrum, to give them a sense that they aren't alone in whatever struggles they face, and to assure them that they can lead happy, healthy, and fulfilled lives.

In addition, this book should result in anyone reading it to gain insight into the unique phenomena that is autism from a mother-son perspective. I also hope that whatever advice is taken from this text will "guide the guides" toward some methods to support their children in becoming self-realized, autonomous, and empowered adults. For those who require higher levels of care, I pray for them to receive care that is of high quality and performed by compassionate professionals. Let's work together to make sure that everyone who needs care gets it, regardless of any social, economic, or political circumstance.

I realize how fortunate I am. If my parents and professionals had not been willing and able to help me in the ways they did, I doubt that I would have ended up where I am today. Who would have guessed that this "autistic boy" could be on the air, doing hired and volunteer radio and voice work for over seven years, and could write a book?

I hope that my story will serve as an example for how the stereotypes surrounding a diagnosis cannot and will not ever fully prescribe or define who someone is. Clearly, the ways

parents, professionals, and society at large address autism can make all the difference in how able people on the spectrum are able to live happy, fulfilling and meaningful lives just like anyone else.

If you finished reading this book, and are now at the end, you certainly are going in the right direction. If you are a mother guide, let this book serve as a guide for you on your journey to help those in need.

Even though this is just one perspective, and everyone's autism is unique, there are some things we on the spectrum all agree on. I hope that my point of view has given you some insight into how to understand your children and others like them.

And most of all, I wish a happy, fulfilling, and meaningful life for everyone. With love standing by us, advocating, and fighting for us, and helping us advocate and fight for ourselves, that is certainly possible.

Despite some grim predictions for my life, I think I turned out pretty well. With your help, I'm sure that no matter what anyone else says or thinks, your children or loved ones on the spectrum can also turn out well and make their mark on the world. Take it from someone who's been through it; I'm OK, and you're going to be OK, too.

References

Baron-Cohen, Simon. *"The Concept of Neurodiversity Is Dividing the Autism Community."* Scientific American, 30 April 2019. https://blogs.scientificamerican.com/observations/the-concept-of-neurodiversity-is-dividing-the-autism-community/

Center for Disease Control. *"Spotlight On Closing the Racial and Ethnic Gaps in the Identification of Autism Spectrum Disorder among 8-year-old Children."* CDC, 2 December 2021. https://www.cdc.gov/ncbddd/autism/addm-community-report/spotlight-on-closing-racial-gaps.html

Chomhaill, Nadia Nic Giolla. *"Family Of Missing Social Media Star, Carly Fleischmann, Says She Is 'Doing Well.'"* Unwritten, 14 January 2021. https://www.readunwritten.com/2021/01/14/family-missing-carly-fleischmann/

Cohmer, Sean. *"'Autistic Disturbances of Affective Contact' (1943), by Leo Kanner."* Embryo Project Encyclopedia, Arizona State University, 23 May 2014. http://embryo.asu.edu/handle/10776/7895

Kapp, Steven Kenneth. *"Social Justice and Autism: Links to Personality and Advocacy."* Dissertation. University of California, Los Angeles, 2016. https://escholarship.org/uc/item/6fm925m3

Rogge, Nicky, and Juliette Janssen. *"The Economic Costs of Autism Spectrum Disorder: A Literature Review."* Journal of Autism & Developmental Disorders, vol. 49, no. 7, 2019, pp. 2873-2900. https://link.springer.com/article/10.1007%2Fs10803-019-04014-z

Wright, Jessica. *"The Real Reasons Autism Rates Are Up In The U.S."* Scientific American, 3 March 2017. https://www.scientificamerican.com/article/the-real-reasons-autism-rates-are-up-in-the-u-s/

About
Joseph D. Shipman

Joseph D. Shipman was born in 1992 in Mountain Home, Arkansas, and now resides in Jonesboro, Arkansas. Despite grim predictions by some following his diagnosis with autism, Joseph managed to gain recognition for his work on air for numerous radio stations. He still lends his voice to a local non-profit radio station, and he gives his time to various political and social causes, including autism advocacy. Joseph takes interest in playing video games, spending time with friends and family, and studying and talking about various topics including, but not limited to, art, history, and philosophy. Mother's Guide Through Autism, Part II: Through the Eyes of the Guided is Joseph's debut as an author.

Writing Brave Press
547 North Avenue, Suite #173
New Rochelle, NY 10801
www.writingbravepress.com

Distributed by IngramSpark

Cover and Text Design: Karinna Klocko
Copyeditor: Meghan Muldowney & Patricia Lemer
Author Photos: Annika Friedland

Library of Congress Cataloging-in-Publication Data available.
ISBN 978-1-7375639-5-2 (paperback)
ISBN 978-1-7375639-6-9 (ebook)

First Edition